T0355031

THE
GREAT ESCAPE

DANIEL JEAN-LOUIS

WestBow
P R E S S®
A DIVISION OF THOMAS NELSON
& ZONDERVAN

WestBow Press books may be ordered through booksellers or by contacting:

WestBow Press
A Division of Thomas Nelson & Zondervan
1663 Liberty Drive
Bloomington, IN 47403
www.westbowpress.com
844-714-3454

Scripture quotations taken from The Holy Bible, New International
Version® NIV® Copyright © 1973 1978 1984 2011 by Biblica,
Inc. TM. Used by permission. All rights reserved worldwide.

ISBN: 978-1-6642-4335-4 (sc)
ISBN: 978-1-6642-4334-7 (e)

Print information available on the last page.

WestBow Press rev. date: 10/16/2021

FOREWORD

The following pages of the book you're reading are meant solely as a reference for those seeking God's face with their whole heart. It is NOT gospel, but ancient wisdom reserved for those seeking salvation from the sinful ways of life and eternal punishment. Discern thoroughly the words of wisdom in this text and apply it to your everyday life. The results will amaze, astound and humble you. May the spirit of truth be with you on your journey into the light!

IN MEMORIAM

My Dad, Elius Jean-Louis, is also my Spiritual brother in Christ.

Disciple of Jesus who I helped baptize 3 months before he went to glory to be with the Lord.

My Spiritual brother in Christ Charles Larry Avila

Disciple of Jesus who I also helped baptize 2 months before he went to glory to be with the Lord.

My Spiritual brother and sister Jesse Stasher and April Baker who went to glory just a few days ago to be with the Lord.

WHO MAY ASCEND THE MOUNTAIN OF THE LORD?

Who may stand in his Holy place?

1 John 2:4-6 NIV

Whoever says, "I know him," but does not do what he commands is a liar, and the truth is not in that person. But if anyone obeys his word, love for God is truly made complete in them. This is how we know we are in him: Whoever claims to live in him must live as Jesus did.

The Christian life is a life of training us to think and act as Jesus would.

Be truthful to yourself. Are you living your life like Jesus did?

Most People say they love Jesus, but they are not doing and following his teaching. This is a reference book that will challenge readers with scriptures. Do not be like the Pharisees and the people that say they already know everything about God. Seek God with all your heart or do you still want to wait for later?

R.D. Baker asked, "Where are the men?"

You know, our world is full of initiatives designed to **Save Endangered Species**.

In the US alone, there are 93 fish, 76 birds, 67 mammals, & 16 reptiles – all endangered, all needing to be saved.

Today I DON'T want to talk about a **"Save The Whales"** campaign

I want to talk…about a massive testosterone **"Save The Males"** campaign!

Because the endangered species that most frightens me…is rapidly becoming "The Christian Man".

The title of my charge is **"<u>Mountain Moving Men's Ministries</u>"** – which is fantastic!

Because a church full of men with Mountain Moving Faith can change the world!

We want to win this world for Jesus Christ…but "Houston? We have a problem!"

We will never **reach the masses**…if we don't first **reach the men.**

Churches all around the world are seeing huge declines in men.

And the number of men in churches…is growing smaller each year.

The typical worship service in the U.S. draws in a crowd that is 61% female & only 39% male!

(With some churches, it's even higher)

Look around your fellowship at your next church service & count noses.

If most of those noses have *lipstick* below them, your church is in trouble.

Because without exception **growing churches** bring in large numbers of men.

And dying congregations lack a strong male presence & participation

I believe that our biggest mission field for unreached people isn't China, it isn't the Middle East – it's MEN.

Men today have become bored, uncomfortable & passive in church

They would rather play golf than meet with the God of the universe!!

And so, one of our church's greatest challenges is "The missing men"

Question – How do we get Bubba off the couch and into our church?

Question – How do we get the future Mighty Men of God engaged?

Question – Didn't Jesus call us to be *Fishers...Of...MEN*?

So, our mission? To figure out how to get men **into the net**...& keep them from **jumping back into the sea!**

In case you forgot, our church was started by a man & his 12 male associates.

Men must lead this church... *"When the men lead, and the people gladly follow, praise the Lord!"*

And that means we can't ignore men's needs...or devalue their strengths.

Our church can't be overrun by feminine ideals.

Now I love that we have a powerful women's ministry. We need that.

But if your church is predominantly women, don't blame the women or ask them to slow down!

Because what women need…truly need…is **a powerful men's ministry**!

Let's talk about the State of the Male Union right now:

~ Most men dropped out of church as teenagers

~ Many men only attend church the obligatory 3 days a year: Christmas Eve, Easter, & Mother's Day

Men regard going to church like getting a prostate exam: **It's something that can save their lives, but it's so unpleasant and invasive – so they put it off.**

Church is like a weekly dose of religion : something they must swallow to remain healthy – but not something to look forward to!

~ Many men would rather go fishing with a couple of their buddies than come to church.

~ They say they believe in God, call themselves "Christian" & even admit to feeling a strong connection with God, yet fewer & fewer go to church. (Especially highly masculine men, young, athletic men)

Question – Are they in church on Sunday? Nope!

Question – Why? Ask! He'll say, "I can worship God better out in nature…than by sitting in a church building!"

"I just don't feel like I need to go to church to be a good person!"

"Church is boring, and not relevant to my life!" "I don't mind if my wife goes…but it's just not for me!"

And again, these men honestly believe they are Christian but church isn't even on their radar!

They tried it – it didn't work – they're done.

How about this recent poll: In the US, 90% of American men claim to believe in God
~ 5 out of 6 call themselves Christians
~ But just 1½ out of 6 claimed to have attended church in the previous week
"Well, men are just less religious." – Untrue!
Judaism, Buddhism & Hinduism have about equal numbers of men & women congregants.
In the Islamic world, men are publicly and unashamedly religious.

I don't truly believe men hate God or Christ or the Bible or even Christianity…
They hate a church system that's perfectly designed to reach someone else.
No, men aren't ashamed of Christ, they're ashamed of feminization in the church.
Some don't even notice there's a **gender gap** in their church
A gender gap is a church with 12% more women than men (56% of your church is women, 44% are men)

Question – So who goes to church? Women!
In a recent survey the typical churchgoer was a 50-year-old, married, well educated, employed and female.
Another poll says there are more women (61%) than men (39%) in the pews.
Almost a quarter of America's married churchgoing women…regularly attend without their husbands.
Mom may be wearing a nice diamond wedding ring but the man who gave it to her is nowhere to be seen.

And everything I've studied says **the exodus of men** from our church is only getting worse...

Count how many married women come to church without their husbands, yet not one married man comes to church without his wife...

And frankly, there are better offers out there for a man on Sunday mornings.

More & more men let their wives decide which church they will go to.

In some churches the only man in the room who is fully engaged & sold out...is **the evangelist.**

Men are becoming even less committed, they are mute during worship & hardly ever volunteer.

Question – How can so many men who claim to know Christ hate going to church?

Well, I believe it's time to start looking at your church and ask yourself:

Question – Why are the men not coming to my church?

Question – Is my church built to reach women and children?

Here's some research results: Churches in our society are now **engineered to reach women!**

That's a startling truth: Most people think of Jesus as having values that come naturally to a woman.

When you think of these terms, what comes to mind? **Love, communication, beauty, relationships, support, helping, nurturing, feelings, sharing, relating, community, loving cooperation, & personal expression** – These are thought of as feminine traits.

What about these traits? **Competence, power, efficiency, achievement, skills, proving oneself, results, accomplishment, goals, self-sufficiency, success, & competition** – those are manly traits.

If we build our church exclusively on either of these values, it will attract people with those gifts.

Meanwhile people who don't have those values have a harder time going to church.

Why? Because they don't fit in. They don't feel useful or even compatible with Christ.

Somehow Christianity has become – at its core – a soft, nurturing faith (and that does not attract men!).

In this mindset, to be like Christ means always loving, always caring, always compassionate, always gentle. **"Jesus does not judge people, he hugs them!"**

And men pick up **the scent of a woman** in our churches.

Men like to feel masculine...they like to feel manly!

Manliness is not something a man does – it's **who he is**.

And a typical man won't do something he believes is feminine.

Therefore men don't go to baby showers or flower shops or boutiques! ("What will the guys think?").

"Real men" don't go to church on a weeknight!"- That's a female activity!

Really?

How did a religion founded by a man & his 12 rugged male disciples become a 'ladies club' in men's minds?

Sadly, Christian men hide their faith from other men.

I love a church filled with manly men, like me!

DANIEL JEAN-LOUIS

I love hearing Kip McKean preach powerfully about the Mighty Men in the bible.

Sermons about Jesus being a revolutionary, being radical, ruthless, & reckless.

Sermons like "They hated the dreamer!" – is the type of preaching that makes me want to sign up and fight!

A Jesus that I would run through a wall for!

Therefore, I'm so grateful that in this church – we have Tim Kernan, Michael Williamson! Cory Blackwell!

There's nothing effeminate about them. And they attract other strong men. Men who want to win the world.

That's why even at 55, I still get pumped when Raul Moreno challenges, 'Are you a preacher or prophet?'

So how do we begin to change this?

One area is found in <u>Revelation 5:2-7</u> – The elders are looking at the throne & see "the Lion of Judah".

John looks at the same throne & what does he see? "A Lamb"

There's a bit of confusion – until they realize **they are looking at the same Jesus**.

Sometimes we look at Jesus and we see a lion, and other times we look at him and see a Lamb.

But they are **one and the same**.

The problem is that there are two Jesuses that are being preached in our churches:

- One is loving, tender, kind, humble, poor, not aggressive, not combative, turns the other cheek, suffers...

- The other is tough, challenging, radical, wild, a volcanic temper, overturning tables, swinging a whip, expressing impatience with his guys, hurling insults at both friend and foe...

We want our men to behave like the Lamb of God, not the Lion of Judah!
The Lion is like Kamikaze Christianity – the Lion of Judah always leaves a mess!

Lamb-Jesus or Lion Jesus?

Go buy a cheap bible:

~ Take a **pink** highlighter & mark all the passages where Jesus is tender, loving & kind.

~ Then take a **blue** highlighter and mark all the verses where Jesus is tough, challenging, and wild.

You'll be shocked at how much LION you'll find!

The problem is that most churches have locked Lion Jesus in the attic (like some crazy uncle!).

Sermons that only focus on being gentle lambs make people think Jesus had few 'lion-like' moments.

Preachers distancing themselves from the powerful, pulpit-pounding sermons many grew up with...

The result? **Lamb Jesus** is mostly heard, emphasizing Christ's grace, gentleness, love, and humility.

Lambs are MUCH easier to control & much easier to lead than lions!

Question– What leader wants a church full of lions?

Overturning tables at the missions bake sale & warning new members of impending doom?

"It's okay to live in sin!" says the Jesus of no-judgment, no discipline!

"Jesus loves me and would never tell me I'm in sin!"

"A Jesus who makes me feel uncomfortable? That's not Jesus for me!" NO!

"God made this Jesus, whom you crucified BOTH Lord & Christ!"

We are called to be like the founder of Christianity – imitators of him.

Who Jesus is – forms the foundation of our faith!

What do you do when you come across a passage where Jesus is being disagreeable, rude, or aggressive?

Question – Do we skip them or apologize for him? "Oh, he's not usually like this!"

"Temple-clearing Jesus is having a monthly meltdown!"

Question – When the Lion of Judah shows up in your sermons, do people in your church recognize him?

Question – Do we, as evangelists, work hard to tame, condemn, and declaw him?

If you speak too boldly, you might hurt someone's feelings!

Question – Are your sermons filled with the favorite words of our lion: Sin, Repent, Hell?

When people only hear about and believe in the Lamb-Jesus, they expect every experience to be pleasant!

"You know, the baby Jesus grew up!"

Disciples abandon the church over the smallest hurt, wound, or disappointment.

Point out someone's sin? Oh baby! "Lamb Christ would never do that!" Yeah, but "Lion Jesus will!"

"What do you mean I can't live with my girlfriend? I'm outta here! I'll be looking for Lamb Jesus!"

In all seriousness, the result is that people believe so much in God's gentleness, they no longer fear his wrath.

"God is not a judge who holds us accountable for our actions – he is a protector who watches over us!"
He is no longer a disciplining father; he's a doting grandfather. Sad.
Sad because Jesus is BOTH the Lamb AND the Lion, as John discovered in Revelation 5.

<u>Romans 11:22</u> – Simply says, ***"Consider the kindness & sternness of God"***
Hmm? Is God a kind God…or a stern God? The answer is "YES!"
But when we create & preach a half-Jesus, we make him & his church less attractive & less compelling to my half of the human race. **The men!**
The more Christians follow this half-Jesus, the more feminized Christianity becomes.
If we only focus on the gentle side of God, God will become softer in our theology and from our pulpits.
Judgment and wrath disappear and are replaced by mush & goo.

The **Lion of Judah** is like canned spinach:
He's sometimes slimy, unpleasant, & hard to swallow, but he builds muscle – especially in men!
His insane courage, bold truth-telling, and revolutionary zeal ignited a flame in my heart 29 years ago.
I love the Lamb of God, but **I'm intimidated by the Lion of Judah**!

This creates in me a tension that makes Jesus so fascinating to me and to other men.
I want to tell the world about this complete Jesus!
And I hope you do too.
Let's NOT call men back to our church…it's time to call our church back to men!

This book is for religious people that say Jesus is LORD and Savior, but their actions say otherwise.

It will summarize Catholicism and its 1+billion followers; Protestantism and it's 1+billion followers- the Seventh-day Adventists and it's 21.4+ million followers; Latter Day Saints movement (Mormonism) 16.7+ million followers; Jehovah's Witnesses 8.5+ million followers; Ambassadors for Christ =Thousands + Disciples (Restoring the 1st century Church)

The word Disciple is in the Bible over 270 times and the word Christian only 3 times so a Disciple is a Christian, but a Christian might not be a Disciple. A Disciple of Jesus follows everything Jesus said, imitates him, speaks like him, acts like him, studies the Bible with others and turns them to disciples, baptizes so they can do the same for him or her to be a sold-out disciple (Set Apart for God).

Life here is fragile and short so as people we cannot do anything without God. If you think you can, this book might not be for you. We live by faith, hope, and love so by living as such, God gives us wisdom with humility which is one of our greatest virtues. I am convinced all of us need to take the time, if we really want Jesus to be an essential part of our lives, to figure out what God wants to teach us.

Apart from a relationship with God, we can either hold everything inside of us thus hurting ourselves on the inside, or we constantly lash out at people in our life, hurting them because of our discontentment.

It is the separation from God that makes us feel so miserable on the inside. True joy comes from God even in affliction and troubles.

CATHOLICISM

Reality is:

Our LORD and Savior Jesus ascended to the right hand of his Heavenly Father, he invited all of us (that are willing) to his house and be part of his Kingdom. There are millions of people on their knees asking other dead people just like them (they call them Saints) for permission if they can go inside.

Here is a list of Their Sacraments

Infant Baptism:

Babies do not have "original Sin" The scriptures say:

Ezekiel 18:20 NIV

The one who sins is the one who will die. The child will not share the guilt of the parent, nor will the parent share the guilt of the child. The righteousness of the righteous will be credited to them, and the wickedness of the wicked will be charged against them.

Colossians 2:12 NIV

having been buried with him in baptism, in which you were also raised with him through your faith in the working of God, who raised him from the dead.

Babies do not have "Original Sin". They do not have faith to call on the name of Jesus, they are innocent in the eyes of the LORD. They are saved at baptism through faith therefore it's a grown-up decision not a baby.

The Eucharist or First Communion:

Because of a lack of knowledge, they believe it becomes the true "flesh and blood" of Christ after it is blessed by the Priest.

The Catholic Church declares that the presence of Christ in the Eucharist is true, real, and substantial. The presence of Christ in the Eucharist is substantial, that is, involving the underlying substance, not the appearances of bread and wine. 22% of them do not believe that.

The scripture says:

John 6: 55-56 NIV

For my flesh is real food and my blood is real drink. Whoever eats my flesh and drinks my blood remains in me, and I in them.

Can a divided home stand? Many of their followers believe that Jesus is talking about the Word of God.

Scripture also says:

Whenever you do Communion, you proclaim the Lord's death, until he comes.

Confirmation:

A retroactive faith. The decision was made by somebody else (Someone was baptized as a baby and now you can become a member.)

Question is: Where is the faith in Jesus Christ that you must have to be part of God's Kingdom?

The scripture says:

Ezekiel 3:20 NIV

Again, when a righteous person turns from their righteousness and does evil, and I put a stumbling block before them, they will die. Since you did not warn them, they will die for their sin. The righteous things that a person did will not be remembered, and I will hold you accountable for their blood.

Penance:

Inflict suffering physically on yourself to bring about righteousness on your account.

Reality is:

It is **malice** because that word is not only to inflict harm or suffering on another but also towards yourself and is glad when bad things happen as a self-punishment. That is not the teaching of Jesus Christ. The scripture says:

Hebrews 9:15 NIV

For this reason, Christ is the mediator of a new covenant, that those who are called may receive the promised eternal inheritance—now that he has died as a ransom to set them free from the sins committed under the first covenant.

HOLY ORDERS

According to its doctrine, not everyone is a part of the priesthood.

Reality is:

Everyone who is saved is a Saint, and everyone who is saved is part of the Kingdom of God

The scripture says:

1 Peter 2: 9 NIV

But you are a chosen people, a royal priesthood, a holy nation, God's special possession, that you may declare the praises of him who called you out of darkness into his wonderful light.

Marriage-Celibate Priesthood.

It is a good thing for a man and woman to be married and must stay faithful. Here what the scriptures say:

1 Timothy 4:1-3 NIV

The Spirit clearly says that in later times some will abandon the faith and follow deceiving spirits and things taught by demons. Such teachings come through hypocritical liars, whose consciences have been seared with a hot iron. They forbid people to marry and order them to abstain from certain foods, which God created to be received with thanksgiving by those who believe and who know the truth.

The Anointing of the sick:

Must be performed by a priest according to Catholicism.

Reality is:

The letter was written for disciples of Christ.

James 5:13-14 NIV

Is anyone among you in trouble? Let them pray. Is anyone happy? Let them sing songs of praise. Is anyone among you sick? Let them call the elders of the church to pray over them and anoint them with oil in the name of the Lord.

The Vatican uses scriptures that are convenient for them.

ADORATION OF THE VIRGIN MARY

They preach that she was born without sin and ascended into heaven

Reality is:

Mary had other children, so we must treat her with respect. Just don't worship her, only God!

Scriptures say:

Mark 3:31-35 NIV

Then Jesus' mother and brothers arrived. Standing outside, they sent someone in to call him. A crowd was sitting around him, and they told him, "Your mother and brothers are outside looking for you." "Who are my mother and my brothers?" he asked. Then he looked at those seated in a circle around him and said, "Here are my mother and my brothers! Whoever does God's will is my brother and sister and mother.

Luke 11:27-28 NIV

As Jesus was saying these things, a woman in the crowd called out, "Blessed is the mother who gave you birth and nursed you." He replied, "Blessed rather are those who hear the word of God and obey it.

The Rosary-

Worship of a Woman/Mother goddess in Paganism is common. People like the idea of praying to Mother Mary.

The scripture says:

Matthew 6:7-8 NIV

And when you pray, do not keep on babbling like pagans, for they think they will be heard because of their many words. Do not be like them, for your father knows what you need before you ask him.

THE CANONIZATION
OF SAINTS-

The declaration of a deceased person as an officially recognized saint.

Reality is:

This is not permitted in the Old Testament or in the New Testament! The Scriptures say:

Leviticus 19:31 NIV

Do not turn to mediums or seek out spirits, for you will be defiled by them. I am the Lord your God.

... The blood of Jesus makes us pure before God. He does not see us for what we are but what we could be, so our life will change when we start living for God instead of our earthly desires. We must obey God rather than human beings!

Unfortunately, most people will not change so they will die for what they are now.

Holy days of Obligation:

Their followers are obliged to participate in the Mass, and they are to abstain from those works and affairs which hinder the worship to be rendered to God.

Reality is:

We should always follow the word of God instead of men. Scripture says:

Galatians 4:9-11 NIV

Now that you know God—or rather are known by God—how is it that you are turning back to those weak and miserable forces? Do you wish to be enslaved by them all over again? You are observing special days and months and seasons and years! I fear for you, that somehow, I have wasted my efforts on you.

Purgatory- The concept that people need to be purged or purified of their sin before they go to heaven.

Reality is:

When someone dies with their sins unforgiven, they have only hell to look forward to.

The scripture says:

Matthew 10: 28 NIV

Do not be afraid of those who kill the body but cannot kill the soul. Rather, be afraid of the One who can destroy both soul and body in hell.

Conclusion

Most religious people are born into their denomination and follow it. God gives all of us knowledge and the ability to ask questions. Sincerity does not equal truth! The only way to follow Jesus is by the words of Jesus not by what someone else told you. Please escape and study the Bible with all your heart then the LORD can reveal himself to you and be holy in his sight.

JEHOVAH WITNESS

Reality is:

They refuse to believe that God's power is so great that his Spirit became flesh and blood to save us, guide us and take us to his Heavenly Father. Christians refute their beliefs with scriptures but on some occasions because of their mistranslated Scripture they call the New World Translation it's hard for them to comprehend the truth.

They stand on men made not of historic faith. There will be no plea of ignorance because they are following a doctrine that started in 1870 instead of the only true church left by our brother's first century church.

What is so curious about their bible even in their translation, it is obvious who the Son of Man is.

Nobody comprehends the Trinity- We can agree to it from an intellectual standpoint, but we know the Spirit of God 100% is on them, God is Spirit! Blessed are those who believe in the Son of Man. Believe in what he said and do the will of his father. Those people will be called "Children of God"

We also don't comprehend eternity- God is the beginning, middle and end! Once again, we can agree to it from an intellectual standpoint but not fully comprehend it.

Isaiah 55:8-9 NIV

For my thoughts are not your thoughts, neither are your ways my ways," declares the Lord. "As the heavens are higher than the earth, so are my ways higher than your ways and my thoughts than your thoughts.

First Core Belief: they do believe that Jesus Christ died for humankind's sins, ***however they do not believe that he was physically resurrected after his crucifixion.*** Not enough to misinterpret the Bible, they have also mistranslated it. The Scripture says:

Luke 24:38-39 NIV

He said to them, "Why are you troubled, and why do doubts rise in your minds? Look at my hands and my feet. It is me! Touch me and see; a ghost does not have flesh and bones, as you see I have.

Second Core Belief: Jesus is not God; he is a god! The scripture says: The Word was God but in their translation the Word was a god.

Jesus is not simply a creation of God but in fact God- the creator Himself

Ezekiel 34:15 NIV

I myself will tend my sheep and have them lie down, declares the Sovereign Lord.

They are contradicting themselves because they also acknowledge there is only one God.

They believe Jesus Christ was the archangel Michael in his previous state and the brother of Satan himself.… Mormons believe this as well!

Will you go by the word of God or the devil?

They are trying to understand the non-understandable and so they change it to make it understandable. There are things in the Bible we as humans cannot comprehend… This should give us more faith in the scriptures because God's thoughts are higher than our thoughts.

Third Core Belief: Steps of Salvation- to have faith, repent, get baptized and persevere to the end to be saved! Good 1st step but the problem is what they baptized into.

A made-up question they ask before baptism.

On the basis of the sacrifice of Jesus Christ, have you repented of your sins and dedicated yourself to Jehovah to do his will?

Do you understand that your dedication and baptism identify you as one of Jehovah's Witnesses in association with God's spirit- directed organization? You are baptized into the Jehovah's Witness Church.

The Scripture says:

Matthew 28:19-20 NIV

Therefore, go and make disciples of all nations, baptizing them in the name of the Father and of the Son and of the Holy Spirit, and teaching them to obey everything I have commanded you. And surely, I am with you always, to the very end of the age.

Fourth Core Belief: Eternity-

They believe only 144.000 anointed men will be saved (They took the numbers in Revelation literally) The scripture does not explain the number but (12 times 12= 144). 12 represents the tribes in the Old Testament and the other 12 represent the apostles in the New Testament.

Revelation 7:4 NIV

Then I heard the number of those who were sealed: 144,000 from all the tribes of Israel.

The big number is symbolic for the whole people of God under both the New and Old Covenant.... Not to be taken literally! If we were to take this passage literal then technically speaking, these (144,000) must not have had sex or touched woman.

HELL: ANNIHILATION

Not a place of torment, but a fire you are immediately destroyed in.

The scripture says: There is eternal punishment, day and night torment for those in hell.

You take away hell as an eternal punishment and you take away one of the primary motivations which is the fear of God.

Matthew 25:41 NIV

Then he will say to those on his left, 'Depart from me, you who are cursed, into the eternal fire prepared for the devil and his angels.

Fifth Core Belief: Prophecies-

They have prophesied over and over when Jesus would come back. *In 1914 they prophesied that Jesus would return but since it didn't happen, they said he would come back in secret and established a "Secret Kingdom"*

There is no "secret" second coming of Jesus. Scripture says:

Revelation 1:7 NIV

Look, he is coming with the clouds," and "every eye will see him, even those who pierced him"; and all peoples on earth "will mourn because of him." So shall it be! Amen.

Here are a few scriptures that tell us who the Son of Man is.

God raised Jesus from the dead

1 Corinthians 6:14 NIV

By his power God raised the Lord from the dead, and he will raise us also.

The Holy Spirit raised Jesus from the dead

Romans 8:11 NIV

And if the Spirit of him who raised Jesus from the dead is living in you, he who raised Christ from the dead will also give life to your mortal bodies because of his Spirit who lives in you.

Jesus raised himself from the dead

John 10:18 NIV

No one takes it from me, but I lay it down of my own accord. I have authority to lay it down and authority to take it up again. This command I received from my father.

Isaiah 9:6 NIV

For to us a child is born, to us a son is given, and the government will be on his shoulders. And he will be called Wonderful Counselor, **Mighty God,** Everlasting Father, Prince of Peace

Ask their leaders what the scripture above means and if the answer is not as clear as the scripture. Ask them if God is trying to confuse us.

Psalms 32:9 NIV

Do not be like the horse or the mule, which have no understanding but must be controlled by bit and bridle or they will not come to you.

MORMONISM

Reality is:

Let's have their own Core Belief for Salvation speaks against them: "Jesus is our redeemer through faith in God, Jesus, and Joseph his prophet, and Brigham is his successor, and you will be saved in his Kingdom" James Talmage, Articles of First, pp85,91

Ephesians 4:5-6 NIV

One Lord, one faith, one baptism; one God and Father of all, who is over all and through all and in all.

Reality is:

For you to be saved, you must be baptized in the name of the Father, the Son and the Holy Spirit. They are all in agreement because they are One.

Joseph Smith Jr. founder of the Mormon Church received his first vision according to his writings in 1820 and 1823 he received his second vision from "The Angel Moroni" who had him transfer words from a golden plate into a book, which became known as the Mormon Book

Three years after the death of Joseph, Brigham Young got rid of polygamy and some of the more controversial teachings to make it more socially acceptable.

Today there are 2 main different Mormon groups:

1. **Reformers/ Fundamentalist-** Hold on to all of Joseph Smiths teaching including polygamy but are often in hiding because of illegal behavior.
2. **LDS (Latter-day Saints)-** hold Brigham Young watered down more palatable version of Joseph Smith's teachings!

We will focus on the latter because it's the one that is still effectively spreading!

First Core Belief: There are many gods-

They claim to believe in the Trinity, but their goal is to become a god and Jesus is not the only son of God, but we are all brothers and sisters of Jesus and therefore one of us could have been Jesus. One of the claims they have in common with Jehovah Witnesses is that Satan was Jesus' brother.

"Here then, is eternal life- to know the only

The scripture says:

Galatians 1:8 NIV

But even if we or an angel from heaven should preach a gospel other than the one we preached to you, let them be under God's curse!

Another revelation from an angel or someone else is in fact another gospel.

All teachings from apostles must support the teachings of Jesus instead of contradicting them, like Mormonism. There is only one God, Jesus is the one God. Jesus is the exact representation of God the scripture says, so why is that so hard to understand when people say they believe the scripture?

Joseph could have been telling the truth, he really saw an angel, but that doesn't mean the angel told the truth!

Satan can masquerade himself as an angel of light.

Hebrews 1:3 NIV

The Son is the radiance of God's glory and the exact representation of his being, sustaining all things by his powerful words. After he had provided purification for sins, he sat down at the right hand of the Majesty in heaven.

Second Core Belief: Salvation-

They teach faith, repentance, baptism and perseverance so the timeline will not work with them.

"Jesus is our redeemer through faith in God, Jesus, and Joseph his prophet, and Brigham is his successor, and you will be saved in his Kingdom" James Talmage, Articles of First, pp85,91

There is no Hell according to them, only 3 Levels of Heaven and that everyone in the world will eventually end up in one of them!

Jesus teaches on hell and destruction in 46 verses, he also uses the word hell 16 times

Clearly Jesus believed in a literal hell

Third Core Belief: Marriage in Heaven-

They teach that in heaven, or in your celestial planets, you will be married to many wives! The goal of Mormonism is that you get up to the third heaven, with your own planet, being your own god, with your own wives starting a celestial life on your own!

The scripture says:

Mark 12:24-25 NIV

Jesus replied, "Are you not in error because you do not know the Scriptures or the power of God? When the dead rise, they will neither marry nor be given in marriage; they will be like the angels in heaven.

Mormonism is a doctrine that was fabricated by the will of a young man named Joseph Smith. He created it to augment his lustful desires through polygamy. Mormons claim that the Book of Mormon is the most accurate book ever written, yet it has gone under 3,000 significant changes since being written in 1830

As a member if you sell a house without telling them, they will find out and expect a tithe from it.

Archeological Evidence still proves Mormon facts false:

1) No Book of Mormon cities have been located.
2) No Book of Mormon names have been found in New World Inscriptions
3) No genuine inscriptions have been found in America of Egyptian or anything like Egyptian, which could correspond to Joseph Smith's "Reformed Egyptian"
4) No ancient copies of the Book of Mormon scriptures have been found
5) No mention of Book of Mormon persons, nations, or places have been found
6) No artificial of any kind, which demonstrates the Book of Mormon is true, have been found
7) To conclude: The Book of Mormon, whether delivered by an angel or fabricated by Joseph Smith's imagination, is a fraud! It is a foundation that is built on lies as its founder, Satan, is a liar!

Joseph Smith was killed at 39 years old, so Mormons consider him a martyr. Who really was the man? He was known as a man of mistress before he invented his doctrine.

He was rumored to have been motivated in part to simply convince his wife that polygamy was of God.

He wrote the "Pearl of Great Price" in part to convince his wife.

Polygamy has attracted many perverts around the world. Joseph struggled with lust so he created a doctrine that would augment his lustful desires… polygamy

2 Peter 1:20-21 NIV

Above all, you must understand that no prophecy of Scripture came about by the prophet's own interpretation of things. For prophecy never had its origin in the human will, but prophets, though human, spoke from God as they were carried along by the Holy Spirit.

SEVENTH- DAY ADVENTISM

Reality is:

Christians have in Christ from what our LORD Jesus told us that faith in Christ and love in our hearts are what matter. What lies beneath the teaching of the Seventh -day Adventist is worrisome! "The Clear Word" is the Bible they use but not officially endorsed; On the surface they seem to preach the Gospel of Jesus but pay attention and listen.

Ellen G. White (their prophetess) said "Jesus is God= 1 point over Jehovah Witness then she openly teaches that Jesus is not God Almighty= 0

All of them must believe that otherwise they are contradicting themselves and following the teachings of a liar. As believers, we should follow the scriptures without getting an explanation somewhere else. The LORD said if you see me, you see my father and again Isaiah said, "a Son will be born, and he will be called Mighty God" the only response is for us to get on our knees before our God the father and his beloved son Jesus and said, "Speak LORD for your servant is listening" Answers will be revealed one day but now We are servants and must only serve.1 Corinthians 4:6 told us not to go beyond what is written so anything after Revelation 22:21 the last verse in the bible is beyond that includes the teaching of Ellen White.

Seventh- day Adventist members believe that God worked through her (Ellen White) in a singular way to clarify and emphasize the Bible's message about Jesus' return. Christians know that God does not clarify his Word through prophets anymore. The Holy Bible speaks for itself. The Seventh Day Adventist considered Mrs. White to be a true prophetess of God.

The choice seems an easy one: Ellen G White or the Holy Bible? Do not be lukewarm, pick one!

Hebrews 1:1-2 NIV

In the past God spoke to our ancestors through the prophets at many times and in various ways, but in these last days he has spoken to us by his Son, whom he appointed heir of all things, and through whom also he made the universe.

The Seventh-day Adventist believes that baptism is a symbol of one's union with Christ, but the fact Is: Baptism is not just a symbol. Rather, it is a person's literal participation in the death, burial, and resurrection of Jesus.

History:

William Miller, their founder, wanted to explain the unexplainable so after studying the book of Daniel concluded Christ's return would be October 22,1844! The Millerite (Miller's followers) were devastated when the prediction did not come to pass. Years later some of them did not give up, they were still looking for a new prophet. Here came **Ellen G. White.**

Ellen and her husband wrote a magazine called "The Present Truth" which is now called "The Adventist Review"

Ellen G. White:

White claimed to have received over 2,000 visions and dreams from God. No vision is from God if it does not come from God.

Visions from God or epileptic seizures?

At age nine Ellen received a projectile-type blunt injury to the nasal area of the face and fell to the ground. **Dr. Delbert Hodder,** a pediatrician and active Adventist living in Connecticut. His answer to the title's question is that Ellen White's visions were not visions but can be explained as a unique form of epilepsy known as complex partial seizure. According to Hodder, the many visions White had during her lifetime are regarded as proof she was a prophet but speculates the visions had no supernatural cause.

The Writings of Ellen White: One of the Seventh Day Adventist pastors, Walter Rea, claimed that Ellen plagiarized several other writers. Besides that, through my research, she also contradicted the Bible dozens of times:

"The man Christ Jesus was not the Lord God Almighty." (1903, ms 150, SDA Commentary V, p.1129)

Ellen G. White

In 1873 Ellen G. White contradicted the Bible when she said Elijah was fed by an angel. Then three years later in 1876 she changed her mind and agreed with the Bible that it really was a raven. Then, a year after her death, her editors tried to smooth things over by omitting any reference to either an angel or a raven -- they changed EGW's words to say Elijah was just "miraculously provided with food" (Prophets and Kings, p. 129 written in 1916).

WHILE TEMPTING JESUS, DID SATAN CLAIM TO BE THE ANGEL WHO HAD SAVED ISAAC FROM CERTAIN DEATH?

Ellen G. White: YES. "As soon as the long fast of Christ commenced in the wilderness, Satan was at hand with his temptations. He ... tried to make Christ believe that God did not require Him to pass through self-denial and the sufferings He anticipated. ... He (Satan) also stated he was the angel that stayed the hand of Abraham as the knife was raised to slay Isaac" (Selected Messages, vol. 1, p. 273).

2 Corinthians 11:3 NIV

But I am afraid that just as Eve was deceived by the serpent's cunning, your minds may somehow be led astray from your sincere and pure devotion to Christ.

The Sabbath Day:

It was a gift from God, but people turned it into a burden. Jesus Christ is our Sabbath day today, in whom we rest for salvation.

Observing the Sabbath

...Was a reminder to the (physical) Israel of their bondage and deliverance in Egypt. It was given as a commandment to them as a shadow of things to come, which is the body of Christ.

Matthew 12:8 NIV

For the Son of Man is Lord of the Sabbath.".

The law was done away with Jesus's death, it was nailed to the Cross.

Romans 14:5-6 NIV

One person considers one day more sacred than another; another considers every day alike. Each of them should be fully convinced in their own mind. Whoever regards one day as special does so to the Lord. Whoever eats meat does so to the Lord, for they give thanks to God; and whoever abstains does so to the Lord and gives thanks to God.

Can you imagine apostle Paul saying these things about murderers or adulterers?

Apostle Paul also said:

Colossians 2:16-17 NIV

Therefore do not let anyone judge you by what you eat or drink, or with regard to a religious festival, a New Moon celebration or a Sabbath day. These are a shadow of the things that were to come; the reality, however, is found in Christ.

Seventh Day Adventist contradicts the passage above because some of them teach anyone who attends church services on Sunday is from the mark of the Beast. The Pharisees and teachers of the law were always harassing Jesus, so nothing changes even today because people still are judging by external standards, not true standards, which are our hearts and actions.

The law was given to Moses for his people, the Israelites. They were God's chosen physical nation before Jesus ascended to Heavens so now God has a Spiritual nation, which is his Church so every day we worshipped God in the name of Jesus Christ, every day is special and when our Lord Jesus comes back then we will enter his rest and his Sabbath.

We cannot pick and choose verses in the Bible that are convenient for us. We should always see Jesus and the gift of God instead of judging. Disciples of Jesus Christ, worship God every day.

Our Lord says that his Father is always working every day and even on Saturday Sabbath and Disciples of Jesus Christ are followers, we imitate him by following his every single word.

Seventh Day Adventist observe the Sabbath on Saturday so who am I to judge? I observe every day so there is nothing wrong with that either. The gospel of Jesus gives us freedom to worship his heavenly father with all our hearts and souls. These are the true worshippers that our God is seeking.

Salvation is by faith only in Jesus Christ and our LORD is also the LORD of the Sabbath. We, as Christians, are workers just like Jesus was when he was here. As long as it is day we must do the work of our King Jesus, night is coming when no one will be able to work anymore, and his children will enter his Sabbath.

Our Savior is always working, so as his servants we also must always work. The time is coming for the people that are hearing his message and not following it! They Will all be exposed.

There is one Church, one Gospel and one LORD so all of us cannot be right, there can only be one.

Colossians 2:14 NIV

Having canceled the charge of our legal indebtedness, which stood against us and condemned us, he has taken it away by nailing it to the cross.

Regarding the Sabbath Jesus said to them:

John 5: 17 NIV

My Father is always at his work to this very day, and I too am working.

My Lord Jesus follows his Father's way, so I will always follow Jesus's way.

Hosea 2:11 NIV

I will stop all her celebrations: her yearly festivals, her New Moons, her Sabbath days—all her appointed festivals.

Jesus told the Pharisees that David and his companions were hungry, and they entered the house of God and ate the consecrated bread which was not lawful for them to do but only for the priests and the priests on Sabbath duty in the temple desecrate the Sabbath and yet are innocent. They are innocent because the Son of Man is the LORD of the Sabbath; otherwise, their actions would have made them guilty. Our LORD desires mercy, not sacrifice.

We need to stop judging by mere appearances but by the truth which is only in Jesus Christ.

He made everything new. We experience a new covenant, a new rest, a new command. The writer of Hebrews wrote by calling this covenant new "God has made the first one obsolete"

Before our LORD came to this world, People had to make sacrifices through the blood of animals every year for their sins and had to be circumcised.

The Pharisees and the teachers of the law could not understand the teaching of Jesus and even right now too many of us are being deceived so if we want to worship God on Saturday do it with the freedom you have on Jesus, and if we want to worship on Sunday and everyday do it with the freedom we have on Jesus.

Most people that observe Saturday Sabbath would be condemned under the law that God gave to Moses because they are not observing it according to their understanding. Freedom is on Jesus because he is our high Priest and mediator. He is looking at our hearts until he comes back so we can enter his Sabbath which is God's rest.

How should a Christian observe the Sabbath?

The day we observe the Sabbath is between You and God. Jesus demonstrated that the Sabbath is a day to do great things. It is not what day to observe it but how to observe it. Sabbath was nailed to the cross along with the law of Moses. The disciples were required to first bring the gospel to the Jews even in Gentile provinces, their purpose was purely evangelistic. Be all things for all people if the gospel is preached. The original intent of the Sabbath was a sign between God and Israel. Jesus fulfilled everything just like he said.

We as Christians have the freedom to worship on any day. Let no one judge you for any Sabbath or holy day act. The Sabbath was a Law for the Jews only. This was a mere shadow of the rest God's people have in Christ Jesus. If you're not in Christ, you don't have the true rest. Christians today observe the Sabbath not under the Law but in Christ Jesus. Paul's position was that the day someone worships is a non-issue. Rome did not make Christians adapt Sundays because the scriptures clearly say that the church met on the first day of the week to break bread and also for tithes and offerings.

There is no command in the New Testament to keep Saturday as the only day to observe the Sabbath; we as Christians observe it every day by doing the will of God. Though the Sabbath is to remember creation and bondage, most Christians worship on Sunday to remember our new creation in Christ and our liberation from sin. We need to focus on Jesus always by following his teachings and do not judge people on how they keep the Sabbath.

Praising God puts all things into perspective. When we lose this focus, we lose sight of God and his power. The deceiver wants division between us, but we must entrust ourselves to God who judges justly. Here are some verses about the Sabbath from the Old and New Testaments that anyone can read and pray so God can help you understand if you are really seeking him with all your heart. Ezekiel 20: 10-12 Hosea 2: 11 Romans 13: 8-10 Romans 14: 5-6 Colossians 2: 16-17 Ephesians 2: 15 just to name a few.

To conclude:

The last word in the Holy Bible is Amen. Don't look for other Prophets (**John the Baptist was the last one)** but instead look for disciples of Jesus Christ so you can live your life here for Christ by believing and accepting his gift. Everything else is meaningless.

2 Corinthians 13:14 NIV

May the grace of the Lord Jesus Christ, and the love of God, and the fellowship of the Holy Spirit be with you all.

Seventh Day Adventist is a diverse movement, and not all SDA groups hold to all the teachings of Ellen G. White. But two facts should give pause to their members: Mrs. White, a teacher of aberrant doctrine, is a co-founder of their church; and their church has its roots in the failed prophecies of William Miller.

PROTESTANTISM

Protestantism is a form of Christianity that originated with the 16th-century Reformation, a movement against what its followers perceived to be errors in the Catholic Church. There are over 45,000 denominations that rose from the Reformation. Below is a list of the most common.

Baptist- Lutheran- Methodist- Anglican- Pentecostal- Anabaptists- Protestant- Eastern Orthodox Church- Quakers- Presbyterianism- Assemblies of God- Southern Baptist Convention- Episcopal Church- Evangelicalism- Church of England- Seventh-day Adventist Church- Calvinism- Adventists- Jehovah's Witnesses- Mormonism- Church of the Nazarene- Church of God- United Methodist Church- Continental Reformed church- Nondenominational Christianity

Reality is:

An atheist does not believe and does not have faith. Religious people do believe but have inaccurate faith therefore there is no difference between them. The scripture says:

Revelation 22:10-11 NIV

Then he told me, "Do not seal up the words of the prophecy on this scroll, because the time is near. Let the one who does wrong continue to do wrong; let the vile person continue to be vile; let the one who does right continue to do right; and let the holy person continue to be holy.

Pray Jesus in your heart:

Radio and Television are leading so many people in the wrong direction.

Reality is:

The sinner's prayer is no way to salvation, we must be born again by repent and be baptized then walk in the light and live the rest of your life like Jesus did. Revelation 3:20 is when Jesus said "If anyone hears my voice and opens the door, I will come in" is taken out of context. This verse is addressed to Christians also known as Disciples of Jesus Christ.

That fairy tale of praying Jesus in your heart began in the early 1800's in America.

Romans 10:13 NIV

For, "Everyone who calls on the name of the Lord will be saved.

but ignore the rest of it:

Romans 10:14-15 NIV

How, then, can they call on the one they have not believed in? And how can they believe in the one of whom they have not heard? And how can they hear without someone preaching to them? And how can anyone preach unless they are sent? As it is written: "How beautiful are the feet of those who bring good news!

Jesus Christ sent his Disciples to preach the Gospel to people, make them Disciples, baptize them, and teach them to do likewise.

Baptism:

Some preach that there is no need for it and others preach no need to immerse in water just a sprinkle of water will do.

Reality is:

There is no New Testament conversion when the subject does not get baptized. The definition of immersion is to dip or put something completely into a liquid, or to totally absorb yourself in a particular activity.

It is a person's literal participation in the death, burial, and resurrection of Jesus. That is the time you are saved and receive the gift of the Holy Spirit.

Scriptures say.

John 3:5 NIV

Jesus answered, "Very truly I tell you, no one can enter the kingdom of God unless they are born of water and the Spirit.

Acts 8:36 NIV

As they traveled along the road, they came to some water and the eunuch said, "Look, here is water. What can stand in the way of my being baptized?

1 Peter 3:21 NIV

and this water symbolizes baptism that now saves you also—not the removal of dirt from the body but the pledge of a clear conscience toward God. It saves you by the resurrection of Jesus Christ,

Southern Baptist Convention

Founders claimed that, according to the Bible, slavery was "an institution of heaven." They pushed the idea that Black people were descended from the Biblical figure Ham, Noah's cursed son, and that their subjugation was therefore divinely ordained.

God promises wealth and health to every believer:

That is not Jesus's gospel but someone else's.

Christian life will continue to have its challenges including money no matter how faithful we are as Christians.

Our confidence and feelings of security must come from God not from people or personal success.

Reality is:

The Lord knows that we need food, clothes, and a place to sleep in this world and even if we are deprived of all those things, he wants to know if we would still choose him. Do not go after physical satisfaction, prestige but poverty, sorrow and even death come. Stay faithful to the end.

Don't worry about life, food or what we will wear because God will always take care of his children.

Revelation 3:17 NIV

You say, 'I am rich; I have acquired wealth and do not need a thing.' But you do not realize that you are wretched, pitiful, poor, blind and naked.

SPEAKING IN TONGUES

Reality is:

You are glorifying yourself and not God.

1 Corinthians 14:18-19 NIV

I thank God that I speak in tongues more than all of you. But in the church, I would rather speak five intelligible words to instruct others than ten thousand words in a tongue.

Some people believe in God but no Jesus

Jesus said in Matthew 18:3 unless you change and become like a little child, you will never enter the kingdom of God. Many people think that they know better so therefore they think that their opinion is correct. No empathy so they lack the highest form of knowledge.

Zechariah 12:10 NIV

And I will pour out on the house of David and the inhabitants of Jerusalem a spirit of grace and supplication. They will look on me, the one they have pierced, and they will mourn for him as one mourns for an only child and grieves bitterly for him as one grieves for a firstborn son.

I used to live for God but not anymore

There is a disturbing evil that I am witnessing under the sun. People that used to love God so much are now willingly putting down their Spiritual swords and shields to stop fighting on the side of righteousness. They are instead enjoying the company of those that are destined for destruction.

Come now! Let us settle the matter, says the Lord. What wrong have I done to you? When you were being refined on the fire, I was there with you but instead of lifting up your heads calling on me, You threw away the heart of flesh that I gave you and took back the heart of stone. The door is still open, but for how long? In case you don't pick up your Spiritual swords and shields, there will be a Spiritual Scripture on your tombstones.

2 Peter 2:22

Of them the proverbs are true: "A dog returns to its vomit," and, "A sow that is washed returns to her wallowing in the mud."

I am Spiritual, No need for church

Reality is:

Can you be married but never go home to your spouse?

People that talk like that are selfish otherwise they would want to give glory to God with our brothers and

sisters. The church is a Spiritual hospital, but they do not want to get well or worse they don't even realize that they are Spiritually blind, Spiritually Lame and Spiritually withered.

They have a very high opinion of themselves, but they don't realize that our opinion is really the lowest form of human knowledge. It requires no accountability and no understanding.

The highest form of knowledge is empathy for it requires us to suspend our egos and live in another's world. It requires a profound purpose larger than our understanding.

It is in the Church that the Christian Faith is proclaimed and maintained. It is through the Church that an individual is nurtured in the Faith.

Otherwise sooner or later their selfishness will turn to bitterness that will contribute to contempt. The deceiver is also very patient because he knows that he has plenty of time to get to us if we are not protected by a loving family. There is no long ranger disciple, no division, no separation. We must be united, God's nation, God's people which is God's temple.

Jesus poured himself out! Blood and water from his side, to have the bride, the church so that we can pour ourselves out!

The scripture says:

Colossians 1:13-14 NIV

For he has rescued us from the dominion of darkness and brought us into the kingdom of the Son he loves, in whom we have redemption, the forgiveness of sins.

I am a good person:

I help people, I give money and time, I pray every day, I go to church. What else do I need to do?

Reality is:

God wants everything in our hearts to be revealed. God can change everything, including our feelings and memories about the past.

We have all the equipment to go fight but we are not fighting. We might be good people, but we need to be more. Pick up our Cross and follow the Lord so we can be holy. Most likely we are not being led by a true leader. In case your church is not following all the teachings of Jesus Christ, you must run and escape for your life. Not following all the Lord's commands means you will also be axed from God's will. The word of God will always give us the power to overcome the enemy-Satan. The mission is to believe and evangelize.

Scripture says:

Matthew 16: 24 NIV

Then Jesus said to his disciples, "Whoever wants to be my disciple must deny themselves and take up their cross and follow me.

SEX WITHOUT BEING MARRIED/ SAME SEX RELATIONSHIP

Reality is.

The Lord God created us with free will but know this: if you are participating in ungodly behavior and/ or practice same sex relationships, keep in mind you are pleasing yourself not living to please God.

Those who love what is good, what is beneficial, what is honorable must hate what is evil, what is harmful, what is deplorable. We are defined by the things we love as well as the things we loathe. What is true of God is subsequently true of us. For God to love he must also hate.

Romans 1:27-28 NIV

In the same way the men also abandoned natural relations with women and were inflamed with lust for one another. Men committed shameful acts with other men and received in themselves the due penalty for their error. Furthermore, just as they did not think it worthwhile to retain the knowledge of God, God gave them over to a depraved mind, so that they do what ought not to be done.

Marriage should be honored by all, not some. God will judge adulterers, the sexually immoral, same sex sexual relationships, people that are living together and are not married, boyfriends & girlfriends that are feeding their fleshly desires. It is impossible to have a relationship with God if you are one of these people.

Human beings are sexual beings. We are far more than that, of course, but we are not less. Our sexuality is a part of who and what we are, a good gift of God given to bind together a husband and wife to subdue, rule and multiply. Marriage is a gift from God, and we should always want to be unified. Our mission is to be faithful and encourage one another. Like everything else we have, our sexuality is a gift given to us in trust. We are to steward it faithfully, to use it in the ways God commands and to refuse to use it in the ways he forbids. God stipulates that sex is to exist only in the marriage of one man to one woman. As a man, I need to see my wife the way God sees her. Precious because she is God's child therefore not only is God my father, but he is also my father-in-law.

I married a sinner but my wife also married a sinner so Jesus calls on me to love my wife the way he loves the church so therefore I must love our differences: Physical, emotional and rational. Not dwelling on differences. God is and should always be sovereign in my marriage and a cord of 3 strings is not easily broken.

God loves when human beings use the gift of sexuality in the ways he commands, but then necessarily hates it when they abuse it in other ways. Does your relationship bring glory to God? I am sure that you can answer that question. God opposes the proud and the people that cannot submit everything to him. God hates sexual sin, he hates any defilement of the gift of sexuality, and he hates any dishonoring marriage, the only right context for sexuality.

Every other sin a person commits is outside the body, but the sexually immoral person sins against his own body. Biblical scholars debate the meaning of the words but this much is clear: Sexual sin makes a mockery of the significant physical and spiritual union bound up in the sexual relationship. As the Reformation Study Bible points out, "in Paul's teaching, the physical union involved in sexual immorality has special consequences because it interferes with our Christian identity as people who have been united with Christ through the Holy Spirit." Those who are united with Christ have no business being united with a prostitute or anyone else to whom they are not married.

Sexual sin degrades and misuses the body which God indwells as his temple.

Hope for the Sexually Immoral

Yet there is hope for even the sexually immoral. Apostle Paul discusses the purpose of God's law and says the law was given for the sexually immoral, [and] men who practice homosexuality. God has made provision for all sinners! The law was graciously given to expose their sin, their desire to sin, and their inability to stop sinning. But, of course, the law was not enough, so Paul immediately switched from the goodness of the law to the goodness of the gospel, to what he refers to as "the gospel of the glory of the blessed God." That gospel insists that none of us are beyond redemption, none of us beyond salvation, if only we will turn to Christ for forgiveness. The saying is trustworthy and deserving of full acceptance, that Christ Jesus came into the world to save sinners. There is no sinner beyond his grace.

THE RULER OF THIS WORLD

Surely you know him because if you are not doing God's will; he is your father! How else can you explain everything that is going on? Here are a few examples:

Kelvin Cochran:

It is a frightening day in the world, especially in the United States when a person cannot express their faith without fears of persecution. Persecution when a fire chief loses his job over expressing his Christian faith.

He was fired from the Atlanta fire department after he wrote a book for members of his church expressing biblical views on sexuality, adultery, and homosexuality.

Byron "Tanner" Cross:

A Virginia teacher was placed on leave after a speech disputing "Biological boy can be a girl and vice versa"

Here is what he said

"I love all of my students, but I will never lie to them regardless of the consequences. I'm a teacher but I serve God first and I will not affirm that a biological boy can be a girl and vice versa because it's against my religion. It's lying to a child, it's abuse to a child, and it's sinning against our God."

I don't know Mr. Cochran & Mr. Cross, but I pray that one day their paths will lead them to Christ Disciples. The scripture says if you hope in the Lord, he will renew your strength.

People persecute others because they are ignorant and religious people do it the most. Jealousy will lead to persecution, then you will become an enemy of God.

HANDICAPPED PEOPLE

People who are born with various birth defects or life circumstances that made them handicapped are not a mistake. God wants his name to be glorified through them. Who they are is still an excellent statement of the perfection of God's creation.

God feels very protective of us because he created us. He sees us as belonging to him.

Many times, a person who has been a victim of several misfortunes feels like they are to blame.

They got down on themselves and convinced themselves that they are under curse for doing wrong in their lives.

Do not lose confidence, God made us perfectly and exactly the way he wanted us. The question is "Do you want to get well?"

Think about the kind of person you would like to be despite the present challenges in your life and then become that.

John 9:2-3 NIV

His disciples asked him, "Rabbi, who sinned, this man or his parents, that he was born blind?" "Neither this man nor his parents sinned," said Jesus, "but this happened so that the works of God might be displayed in him.

ALL YOU MUST DO
IS TO BELIEVE

Reality is:

In order to be part of God's kingdom, you need to do much more than that. The most important one is to love God and do what is right, not what is left. If you keep sinning, realize that you are an enemy of God. When we harbor sins in our heart, we are no different than those who have sinned against us. We need to wake up and let Christ's light shine on us.

James 2:19-20 NIV

You believe that there is one God. Good! Even the demons believe that—and shudder. You foolish person, do you want evidence that faith without deeds is useless?

Lots of people quote the scripture below to justify their evil behavior

Romans 10:9 NIV

If you declare with your mouth, "Jesus is Lord," and believe in your heart that God raised him from the dead, you will be saved.

Suppose that you have a wife that calls to tell you that your baby makes his or her first steps and the baby now can walk. Does that mean the baby can walk like you?

You must read the chapter not only that verse in order to understand what Paul meant by what he said because he was writing to Christians, people that are already following all the teachings of Christ. In case you want to quote a scripture, understand the previous verse first.

Romans 10:8 NIV

But what does it say? "The word is near you; it is in your mouth and in your heart," that is, the message concerning faith that we proclaim:

I REPENTED SO I AM SAVED

Reality is:

In order to be saved you must believe, repent and be baptized. Change your old life completely by living your new life for Jesus. Once you call on Jesus's name as your Lord and your supreme Master, you will be saved if you stay under his Lordship. Do you want to live your life as Jesus did? It is a lifestyle that you must continue to repent by walking to the path of righteousness. You must completely change if the world cannot see any changes in you so you must know that God does not see any changes in you either. You know Jesus you said, but does Jesus know you!

Repentance does not equal salvation. Baptism is the point of salvation; it is a gift from God because of our faith in Jesus knowing that his blood will save us. God needs to forgive you.

Lots of people say that "God cannot hate because he is love" but God hates evil so he must hate because he is all love. Fulfilling the duty of our relationship with God in order to be righteous before God.

DANIEL JEAN-LOUIS

Hebrews 5:11-14 NIV

We have much to say about this, but it is hard to make it clear to you because you no longer try to understand. In fact, though by this time you ought to be teachers, you need someone to teach you the elementary truths of God's word all over again. You need milk, not solid food! Anyone who lives on milk, being still an infant, is not acquainted with the teaching about righteousness. But solid food is for the mature, who by constant use have trained themselves to distinguish good from evil.

We must digest and grow so we can be part of the feast (which is the word of God).

I LOVE GOD BUT IT'S TOO HARD

Reality is:

Not willing to live for God therefore you are not willing to die for him either. When we embrace God's love, we then give it to one another! As he loved us. Not only God told us what love is, but he showed us. It is not enough to tell people what Christianity is, but we must show them if they are willing.

Romans 8:6 NIV

The mind governed by the flesh is death, but the mind governed by the Spirit is life and peace.

Do not destroy your heart in the process of waiting for God's way to unfold.

Jesus stood firm and sacrificed his best for us. His life. It will take sacrifice and decisions to completely overcome just like Jesus. You cannot do God's will if you don't love him

Do not choose lust, malice, lies and deceit instead of God.

Jesus told the people that no one can come to him unless his father has enabled them.

And many of his Disciples stopped following him after Jesus said that. People are being confused and deceived by satan. Our world is Bible illiterate because of the deceiver and that is the reason the church leaders are missing something so obvious. The very last command of Jesus; Go make disciples, baptize them and teach them to do the same.

But if you really want to have a relationship with the Lord, you will realize it's not burdensome but a joy even if you are attracted to the same sex and cannot stay faithful to your spouse or if you're single and you cannot even think of the idea not having sexual relationships.

God loves his children so his Spirit will be inside in order to give you the strength to fight sin in order to be worthy of him. Without Jesus you are your own lord. No one will be able to correct or rebuke you if you have not been taught. Choose God then you will rejoice.

Satan uses the desires of our flesh - Lust- to bring us down. Lust is fearless and does not discriminate. It can be found in both old and young and has no respect for the stature of the individual, social or economic status, background or religious upbringing, it doesn't even care about your skin tone! We all have come face to face with it. What sets us apart is the way we handle it. The enemy uses our fleshly desires and cravings to gain advantage of us if we are not guarded. The desire for sex in this generation is prevalent. In the young and the old, however as Christians we should be aware of the society we live in and its social interests. Today we walk on the streets of the so-called ancient Babylon where Our eyes are triggered to look at everything, whether we come across good or bad.

Our minds are programmed to think we have the "freedom to do whatever we want" to some extent this is true. At the same time it is the gift of freedom we use and find ourselves in temptation which eventually leads to sin, regrets and turning away from God. However, the bible warns us about temptation.

Fleshly desires that look good to our eyes are the source of a dying society and most importantly an abomination in God's kingdom. Giving in to our fleshly desires has been rebellion to God since creation and that has not changed. If we need to succeed on this day, it is crucial that we pray for wisdom and spiritual awareness for the world is blind. Freedom is good as long as we use it to glorify God.

As God's chosen people we are all called to be free, but do not use your freedom to indulge in flesh. Babylon is everywhere we are living in it. What was once a great powerful and affluent city but fell without trace the same is yet to come. Its sin led to its destruction so shall we die away if we aren't free from its leader's agenda. When you think you look good, better than others and don't have any empathy; you must know that you are a descendant of Babylon; God gives us free will to do whatever we want but remember not everything is good for us.

We will go through suffering throughout our lives on earth, meaning crucifying our fleshly desires is part of it, but I want to encourage us that the reward is way more than what the world can provide.

Be faithful, even to the point of death, and I will give your life as your victor's crown.

You are a free being! Free Entry free Exit

SPONTANEOUS BAPTISM

That is really a thing that some Preachers do. How can you baptize someone if that person is not Christ's Disciple?

Reality is:

Here are words of Jesus again:

1 Therefore go and make disciples of all nations,

2 baptizing them in the name of the Father and of the Son and of the Holy Spirit,

Therefore, in order to be saved we must do what the Bible says we should do.

Repent and be baptized, every one of you, in the name of Jesus Christ for the forgiveness of your sins, after that you will receive the gift of the Holy Spirit.

Someone cannot come to you and say they believe, and you baptized them. It does not work that way because you are sending them out to fail before they even get started. There should be studies, repentance and conviction before anyone can be a part of the kingdom of God. Are you ready to get aggressive about the sin in your heart?

Conviction is a "cut to the heart" response to our sin. Coming to conviction is the hardest part of repentance.

Can I really baptize people?

Yes, that is one of the most important commands from our LORD Jesus. Disciples make Disciples. No matter what Denominations, it seems that none of them are following the teachings of Jesus and they are taking you down with them.

Everything the Lord said to his disciples, he also said to us. Some will understand and follow but most will not. Jesus wants us to kill our old life for him to come in and live in us. When you live for Jesus, you will be persecuted but nothing will stick. They might even send you to prison or take your life. Stay faithful always and imitate Christ, the evidence will show by your action.

People like the idea of going to church, paying tithe and being comfortable! How can one follow Jesus without work? Read the Beatitudes in order to weigh your spiritual beliefs.

The scripture says:

Matthew 28:19-20 NIV

Therefore go and make disciples of all nations, baptizing them in the name of the Father and of the Son and of the Holy Spirit, and teaching them to obey everything I have commanded you. And surely, I am with you always, to the very end of the age.

We must always obey God rather than human beings!

I know more than you

It is not about you knowing more or religion, it is about being used by God for the kingdom.

We should be learning and teaching one another in order to do greater things for the kingdom.

The message we should teach to rekindle is the one left by our brothers' first century disciples.

Hate what is evil, hate false doctrine.

Any lowering of what Jesus said is "false doctrine"

Arrogant & Snobbish! Six things the Lord hates, seven that are detestable to him.

Haughty eyes- Lying tongues- Hands that shed innocent blood- A heart that devises wicked schemes- Feet that are quick to rush into evil- False witnesses who pours out lies- A person who stirs up conflict in the community.

I have been looking for a family friend for months because I know he likes to read the Bible and Loves God so I wanted to find him so we can share faith and study the Bible together.

We talked on the phone and made plans to meet so we could pray and do a Bible study. We did the study but unfortunately, he feels like he knows more than me. He told me that he's been reading the Bible for decades. Every single scripture has a meaning and a purpose.

What people don't understand, Bible study is a team sport and if you love God, you will want to share it and study with people.

There is no such thing as "I know more than you." We should read the Bible at face value and not water down the message. There are no prideful people in God's kingdom but only servants, people that humble themselves among the lowest in order to do the will of God.

People have all types of excuses for not obeying Jesus' teachings. A good example they say is "I cannot live my life like Jesus"

Why do I know thousands and thousands that are doing it?

I am humble and poor! I live like a Sheep among Wolves.

I don't have anything except the word of God. I am a sinner; I sin from evil thoughts that come up in my head, but I also fight back by humbling myself before my Lord and asking for forgiveness.

Satan is stopping people from even hearing the truth because if they do; the choice will be clear.

It will be as clear as night and day so they will have to make a choice. I struggle every day so I must stay connected to Christ because there is too much to lose.

Isaiah 6:10 NIV

Make the heart of these people calloused; make their ears dull and close their eyes. Otherwise, they might see with their eyes, hear with their ears, understand with their hearts, and turn and be healed.

Who is sent?

Our Lord Jesus sent Disciples to make Disciples in order to evangelize all nations and it is happening right now. Disciples are known by their love for each other, and they know that the message of condemnation must come first before the message of salvation.

Disciples of Christ hate what is evil and false doctrine. They make radical disciples.

The Gospel of Jesus is not for everyone, God wants everyone to be saved but only a remnant will be saved. Isaiah prophesied it about the Jewish people and it is also the same for the Gentiles. Though the number is like the sand by the sea, only a few will live.

Jesus wants you to kill your old life and live for him because when you live for Jesus you will be persecuted but nothing will stick, they might even kill you and take your life. Where are the men? People would rather watch tv or do anything else instead of going to church regularly so how can you expect to be called children of the living God.

The same Spirit that came at Pentecost is still here among us and wants to do God's will. There were millions of people in Jerusalem but only 3,000 received the message and repented. We need to let the Holy Spirit do his work because most of us choose to live for pleasure instead of God, family instead of God, ourselves instead of God. I am writing about the same God that destroyed earth with water before and swore by his great name that you will be destroyed with fire if you don't turn to his Son and kiss him.

You are not trembling before God because you are not scared, and you are not scared because you don't see the urgency of what is coming. I can understand. If people don't believe in God, of course they will not do his will! You, who say that you love God; How is that you are not doing God's will?

Let me share a little bit of the great love that God has for us. Just like the scriptures say that the devil is accusing us before God, and after Adam & Eve sin, all of us should have gone to the slaughter. Satan would have got his wish but because God's love is above everything else, he did not ask Archangel Michael or another Being to rescue us. He himself became one of us and sacrificed himself to save the few of us that are willing to follow his Heavenly Father's will by putting aside our old selves and declare Jesus is Lord and Savior.

How do you know that you are saved!

The Pharisees and the teachers of the law also thought they were saved but Jesus told us unless our righteousness surpasses the Pharisees, we will certainly not enter the kingdom of heaven.

We can do that by obeying every single command he asks from us, not what is convenient or what our parents, pastors, preachers say we should do but instead make the Bible the only standard in our lives.

WHAT IS THE FEAR
OF THE LORD?

Fearing God is not like fearing pain, but it is a protection from the sin and deceit that we so easily fall into. Our Lord Jesus delighted in fearing God. Fear of the Lord will give us the power of righteousness, faithfulness, and Peace.

When we love God so much we develop a deep respect and gratitude for all he has done for us and by fearing the Lord, we feel secure and have no fear of circumstances. To fear the Lord is to hate evil. Our thinking and reasoning get clouded when there is sin in our heart.

When I am struggling and suffering yet still happy, it is because of the Spirit of God. The Holy Spirit inside me is always jumping with joy, glorifying God.

One must be in love with my Lord Jesus to understand these things.

God loves to endure forever so we should stop trusting in ourselves and our thinking. God is in control. Fear the Lord, we will truly understand God's love and be able to put aside our anger, bitterness and/or lack of trust.

Fear of the Lord is to love God and want to please him.
God is in control so be humble before him.

Our Lord died for us in order to have a relationship
with each one of us. He is knocking at the door! Dare
to answer, dare to make him first in your life, dare to
live for him always, dare to be a fisher of men and teach
them to obey the teaching of our Lord Jesus Christ. That
is our purpose in life.

A person who does not fear the Lord can never rise above
the wickedness of this world.

Lack of knowledge is what keeps most people from truly
seeking God because if the World really knows the side
they are standing on, they will want to enlist in God's
army.

People are not fighting so they don't even realize that
they are in the middle of an intense battle but to the few
that are chosen, I want to encourage you to refute false
doctrines.

We are fighting from a position of victory because our
Lord has already won the battle.

When there is knowledge there is no fear because if God
is with us who can be against us?

The devil is a defeated foe and Jesus gave us authority
over him but unfortunately most of us don't believe.

They call on Jesus's name but don't believe, they don't believe because they have not heard, they have not heard because most people are not preaching the truth, they are not preaching the truth because they are not sent.

It is a mystery that people are not trembling before the LORD for what is soon to take place.

They are living their lives like it was on the day of Noah or worse. Apostle Paul stated that Israel is experiencing a hardening until the full number of Gentiles turn to the Lord with all their hearts, so I am writing to give good news to the people that fear the Lord and are waiting on him.

Israel is growing restless and becoming too fat so the yoke will be removed from his neck.

The Shepherd is calling his Sheep so do not harden your heart, you must live like Jesus did to be a citizen of his Kingdom.

In the scriptures Jesus said" Everything must be fulfilled that is written about me in the Law of Moses, the Prophets and the Psalms. When I read Psalms, I do see my LORD all over the chapters. On Psalm 22, the whole chapter (please read it) is about Jesus' suffering that the Holy Spirit helped David write about 1,000 years before our LORD gave his life upon the cross. On verse 6, Jesus stated that he is a worm and not a man. I had to find out what that is all about, so I Google it.

The answer is astonishing! The Hebrew word used in that verse is "TOLA'ATH" which means a scarlet worm or crimson worm both are the colors of blood. When it's time for the mother crimson worm to have babies, she willingly finds the trunk of a tree or a wooden fencepost.

She attaches her body to the wood and makes a hard crimson shell. Permanently stuck to the wood that the shell can never be removed without tearing her body completely apart and killing her.

After she lays her eggs under her body and the protective shell, the baby worms hatch, they stay under the shell for protection and provide them with food. The babies feed on the living body flesh of the mother!

Few days later when the babies can take care of themselves, the mother dies. Minutes before the mother dies, she oozes a scarlet red dye which not only stains the wood that she is stuck on but also her babies. They are scarlet red for the rest of their lives.

Amazingly after three days, the dead mother crimson worm's body loses its crimson color and turns into a white wax which falls to the ground white like snow.

Isaiah 1:18 NIV

"Come now, let us settle the matter," says the Lord. "Though your sins are like scarlet, they shall be as white as snow; though they are red as crimson, they shall be like wool."

Someone that I have known for many years told him that he believes in God but will obey only if he sees God come down. That is an intelligent rebellion! In the past God overlooked such ignorance but now the Gospel is being preached to the whole world and that is a testimony to all nations.

People are hearing the Gospel and they are rejecting it so the antichrist will be allowed to rise.

People that are asking for proof and evidence will get an illusion to satisfy their cravings.

My Lord Jesus Christ said that "A wicked and adulterous generation asks for a sign, but none will be given except the sign of Jonah." That friend of mine cannot even see Jonah's sign because he is blind, he has eyes to see like you nevertheless he is still blind.

Jesus was in the belly of the earth for 3 days and 3 nights just like Jonah inside the belly of a fish. The People of Nineveh turned to Christ when they heard they were going to be destroyed after 40 days so they repented and were saved. Jerusalem did not repent; in fact they killed the Son of God so 40 days/ years later, they were destroyed. Google 70 AD. 40 years after they killed the Lord of glory.

Matthew 23:37 (NIV)

"Jerusalem, Jerusalem, you who kill the prophets and stone those sent to you, how often I have longed to gather your children together, as a hen gathers her chicks under her wings, and you were not willing.

S.O.S.

What can I do or say to make you understand and obey what I know? There is punishment that will follow for those that don't obey the teaching of Jesus Christ!

You need to know the difference between persevering and enduring.

Bad things do happen to the children of God, but they do not dwell on negative thoughts or spiritual battles, they believe in their Heavenly father by keeping their eyes on the Cross.

The children of satan (You are either a child of God or satan) also endure tremendous pain but where is that Victory because all they have is an illusion. Their purpose is fleshly desire but no hope. Some of them will even say "This is it, there is nothing else"
There is pain in the world and pain also as a child of God so you must choose your pain.

Do your best and God will do the rest, his yoke is easy, and his burden is light.

There are 3 important things that you must have to be called a child of the living God.

Spirit of God, Word of God, and the body of Christ. In your current situation, do you love God or yourself?

I personally want you to know that you will soon meet a disciple of Jesus if you really want to have a relationship with the only God there is and will ever be. Disciples of Jesus are the ones that he sent to this world to rescue the lost and we are being treated like Sheep to be slaughtered, even by our own family members because they think we are strange and weird just for loving God and want to do his will in the name of Jesus every single day. We no longer participate in the things that this world calls 'fun,' but we know certain things are not fun but sin, Therefore we stay away. We are not surprised that people hate us because we know if we are not persecuted that means we are a part of this world as it is our Lord set us apart and we are no longer one of them.

You said that life is not fair but who cheated? We did! God gave us free will.

The same message that I heard and made me fall in love with God is also there for you if you are willing so the judgment that is soon coming on all of us if we don't follow the message that gives us life is our decision and our choice because God does not send us to the eternal fire, we are choosing it if we don't call on Jesus name and live our lives as Jesus did.

The Word of God is so amazing because when you open your heart to listen and follow, God will reveal his face to you, and you will certainly fall in love.

We need to cut the chain of slavery. The battle really takes place in our mind and the word of God is what we need to learn to control it. Grow a deep conviction by having a faith that can move mountains or everything we are doing is in vain. God gives us the choice to choose him or satan. We need to be filled with the Holy Spirit and stop relying on us. Jesus needed the Holy Spirit so how much more do we need it in order to be victorious. Let's all of us imitate Jesus and live like he did otherwise we are not even in the race.

A Christian life is a journey so we need to always stay focused and do God's will. We need to make sacrifices so we can grow, there is no shortcut and no other way. There will be sacrifice and there will be blood so if we are comfortable, we might not be fighting. One question that we all should ask ourselves. Where will our souls be 500 years from now?

Stay faithful every day! Pray for relief and deliverance even if the situation is hopeless because in the end, God always takes care of the people that belong to him.

RETURN GOOD FOR EVIL

There is a nice sound to that but when push comes to shove, we will not be able to stand the fire without a lot of faith that comes only from Jesus. God will test us, will lay burdens on our backs and he will let us go through fire and water but if our faith is built on a rock, we will stay standing up for him to bring us to a place of abundance. God does not tempt us. We are tempted by our own evil desire that gives birth to sin then death will surely come.

Romans 12:19 NIV

Do not take revenge, my dear friends, but leave room for God's wrath, for it is written: "It is mine to avenge; I will repay," says the Lord.

Our faith is like gold that needs to be refined. The refining process can often be difficult and painful.

In the end, our faith will bring glory to God.

Christ's Disciples however know who they are and where they are. They learn how to persevere and sometimes are excited about the challenges because they are confident about the victory.

They get to prepare the way for Jesus.

Most likely whichever denomination you fellowship with is because your parents were doing it, and you grew up following that same religion. The LORD wants you to be curious. What is wrong with that? What is wrong with the original Church that Jesus laid the foundation; Peter, Paul and the other apostles started?

Little children should be curious, that is what you are if you call on his name as your LORD. In case you don't care, or you think it's too hard, you might care about your children. Your teenage daughter would choose a Bible instead of calling boys and your boys would want to lead people to the LORD because it's in their DNA. Aren't you a little curious?

The deceiver knows if he can seduce you then he can reduce you because he is after your destiny and the authority that you have once you are doing God's will.

I don't know much, but I can boast in the name of my LORD Jesus Christ.

Are you desperate? Hopeless? Looking forward to something better?

Get out of the line because the one that you are standing is going straight to the slaughter, lift your head there is another door that Jesus has opened that will lead you to his father. Be bold because he gave you that power to say "I chose life "and repent completely. Instead of going down south you will go up North.

2 Corinthians 6:9-10 NIV

Known, yet regarded as unknown; dying, and yet we live on; beaten, and yet not killed; sorrowful, yet always rejoicing; poor, yet making many rich; having nothing, and yet possessing everything.

Secret thoughts of evil that no one knows, or attitudes against people that are deceitful.

Christ is light! When we are part of Christ, there is nothing hidden. If we are completely in the light, we will not be in want. Most of our deceit comes from believing Satan more than God/Christ.

Whoever your pastor or leader is; they are not leading you to the narrow path because they are not sent. Imagine for an instant you are a baby; you are not corrupt the way you are now. Listen to the word of Jesus instead of your leaders. Jesus said that he was hungry, homeless, in prison in the hospital so how are you going to answer these questions? Right now, perhaps you go to church on Sundays (only 30% in the U.S.) to listen to an entertainer that makes you feel good about yourself. Our Lord also said "Make Disciples and Baptize them" most Christians do say that they are also Disciples of Jesus Christ but unfortunately most of you are not because Disciples make Disciples and teach them to do likewise by living a righteous life for God to separate them from the people that are born to be destroyed.

That is the purpose of all Disciples; if I ask what's your purpose in life, each person in the world can give me a different answer but Christ disciples have one answer "Make Disciples" restore the first century church by making more Disciples for the Lord just as he commanded us to do.

In case your church is not following all our Lord's teaching, you should run away from it and escape for your life. The mission is to evangelize all nations and yes, it is also your mission! Otherwise, you will ax out of God's will. Let your faith be bigger than fear. Billions of people would love to be you right now because if you are reading these words; You still have hope but soon if you don't do anything about the gift that is being handed to you, the door will soon close, and the hope will vanish forever.

Don't be an agnostic or worse an atheist, we are engaged in warfare, the issues of which are life and death, and every day that we are indifferent to our responsibilities is a day lost to the cause of Christ. Commit yourself to Christ, who is the doctrine so you can have eternal life.

We all want to live but not all of us want to do the requirements that can lead us to eternal life.

Here is the first step that everyone must take. Do not go after physical satisfaction, popular acclaim and prestige, however if poverty, humiliation, sorrow and even death come stay faithful my friend and where you headed you will pity those left behind.

We want you to be like a child, be humble and listen. Are you able to get rid of all your resentments, self-pity, and bitterness?

Stop and leave your life of sin. Do not depend on people including spouses, parents, pastors, children but only on God.

There is no way you can take on such a heavy task if you are not in fellowship with your brothers or sisters in Christ constantly throughout the week and if you are not on your knees every day to pray, worship and ask God for wisdom. Lastly be fruitful by making disciples otherwise you will be cut off and thrown into the fire.

Our LORD said that we must be like a child in order to be called "Children of God." Do not only forgive your enemy but you must love them, pray for them and ask God to help them know him as much as you love God. Do you think you have that much faith and love? A disciple of Christ does.

Here is the conclusion of life.

Listen to the following words:

Trust God in uncertain times because you will face them and if you are not mature in God's wisdom, you will not be victorious, and the ruler of this world will swallow you up.

Ecclesiastes 12:13-14 NIV

Now all has been heard; here is the conclusion of the matter: Fear God and keep his commandments, for this is the duty of all mankind. For God will bring every deed into judgment, including every hidden thing, whether it is good or evil.

Warning

The kingdom of darkness is united against Christians. Unfortunately, Christians are not united and that is the reason so many are fighting on the side of evil and don't even know it.

How can someone explain that when a Disciple of Christ asks a Christian from another denomination to study the Bible then gets rejection instead of love, most of the time it comes from members of our own family! The time is now for us to be united upon the one foundation on which the Apostolic church was founded. One church, one Lord; If your name is written on the book of life, you should understand the message I am sending you.

The enemy knows that his time is short, and his purpose is to confuse as many people as he possibly can, but we need to take a standby seeking unification instead of division.

My people you are inside a train that is headed to the ravine, and you've been warned repeatedly. In case you don't have the fear of God, it's okay because I am not writing to you just have another drink and keep having whatever it is you called fun but if you say that you fear God and that you want to do his will so, please pay attention and do not let the deceiver deceives you anymore because that is what he does and that is who he is.

Seek God with all your heart and the One who promised is faithful so you will find him, the following questions are for you to answer. What is your purpose in life? Happiness or Righteousness, which one are you seeking? What do you fear in life? Do you know what our wages are according to the Bible? I will answer that one for you, it is death for our sins. Do you think it is right?

Do you think that you are a good person? How many lies have you told so far in your life? Fornication? Have you used God's name in vain? Would you use a cursed word to describe your mother? People using God's name mix it with filthy things like cursing and fornication is blasphemy.

Despite all these things, we deserved death, but God still wants to save us by showing us mercy. We committed a crime, but God loves us so much because we were like Sheep without a Shepherd, so he had to come down himself and be our Shepherd. He paid the punishment for us with his life and all he is asking in return is "Come and follow me " We all know the story of Noah so you must know that judgment is coming and the time to seek God is now because tomorrow might be too late. Believe, Repent and Baptize so you can live in righteousness.

Fear of God is when you love God and want to do what pleases God.

Is our generation better than the days of Noah or Sodom and Gomorrah?

Answer this question with what you are witnessing or hearing then you should know without a doubt that the day of the Lord is coming. How come that you are not a fisher of men?

Do not only confess and think that you will be saved, but that is also not enough because the Lord Jesus is seeking workers and wants you to be fruitful by being a Disciple and turn others to be Disciples. This should be your main purpose if not your only purpose in life.

The wage of sin is death and that is what we all deserve but God is so amazing that he gave us a way to escape. Every single one of us deserves to be slaughtered but our Lord is so merciful that he opened another door for us through Jesus Christ.

My people, why do you still refuse to open your eyes and see what I see, hear and hear what I hear but not with the eyes and the ears that you have on your head but with the word of God.

Stop sinning and seek to have a relationship with God by putting aside fleshly desires.

Sin these days is the norm because if someone with a boyfriend or girlfriend is not being intimate, most people will ask: What is wrong with you?

Eventually some of them do get married! Not because of the fear of the Lord but because of the fear of this world. This world has a king, and he is the king of darkness.

I was at the store a few days ago and picked up a book that talked about America's favorite preacher. He passed away now but he brought millions of people to the Lord according to what I was reading and what people say about him. Presidents wanted his religious advice.

Who is that man? He must be a great disciple of Jesus Christ! He wrote the Foreword to a great book that I recommend, "Master Plan of Evangelism" I also recommend "DODEKA, by Dr. Timothy C.Kernan" The man also knew about the great commission and how Jesus wants his disciples to live if people decide to follow him in order to inherit eternal life. He didn't share it with his millions of followers because he was not a disciple of Christ so we cannot expect him to teach or show people to live as such.

"Few books have had as great an impact on the cause of world evangelization in our generation as The Master Plan of Evangelism" -Billy Graham

How could he say that about the book when he was not turning the people that he baptized into fishermen?

What I am writing is not new, we read about it every day and the only reason that people are not doing it is because it requires work.

What a missed opportunity on his part and all the preachers that are not teaching my Lord's people how to follow Jesus and let them decide if they want it or not. People must learn after baptism how to live their lives like Jesus did, not baptise them and send them home to be slaughtered by the enemy.

Imagine turning millions and millions of people into real Disciples of Jesus Christ! (Such a beautiful dream of mine)

The guy I am writing about is also your pastor, your church leader because none of them are leading you to the Shepherd but their messages are very entertaining.

The Lord will not judge by what you see with your eyes or hear with your ears. He will judge our hearts with righteousness so everything will be on full display

Apostle Paul said that some people preach out of selfish ambition and envy but others out of goodwill. Sooner or later, everyone will be exposed for what they really are.

AMBASSADORS/
DISCIPLES OF CHRIST

Every Denomination and Faith all Christians
of every name united upon the one foundation
on which the Apostolic church was founded.

Reality is:

God has an individual plan for each one of us. Do you
want to know what it is and follow his words in the Bible
or do you still want to keep living the same life you are
living?

We are a restoration movement not a reform movement.
We are restoring the first century church. It is not a
dream; it is a reality because Thousands are living it
and you too can be part of that life. Christianity is not
a sprint but a marathon. No pain no gain, No Cross-no
Crown.

Friday afternoon two teenage sisters are being picked up
by their friends. Tina's boyfriend is going to take her out
to the movies then he will take her to his house and drive
her back home in the morning. Her nineteen-year-old
older sister Rita will be picked up by her friend Brunise

from church to go eat and study the Bible with someone. Welcome to God's Kingdom.

This is the Kingdom that our Lord Jesus came here to establish and everyone that follows all his teachings is part of his kingdom and are citizens of the kingdom of God because Jesus is our king. We only listen to his teachings and pray every day even for the people that don't like us and even want to hurt us. Jesus suffered so we also must suffer, he lives so we will also live.

We live for him and everything we do is to please our God in the name of Jesus Christ. It is no longer a physical kingdom with only the people of Israel but a spiritual kingdom where it's king died so his people can rise and live because he defeated death rise and live. Everyone is welcome if they are willing to put on their Spiritual Shield, their Spiritual Armor and Fight.

We as disciples are all unworthy servants in the Kingdom of God, we are only doing our duty if we keep our eyes on the Cross our Lord will make us worthy of his Father.

Jeremiah 31: 31-32 NIV

``The days are coming," declares the Lord, "when I will make a new covenant with the people of Israel and with the people of Judah. It will not be like the covenant I made with their ancestors when I took them by the hand to lead them out of Egypt, because they broke my covenant, though I was a husband to them," declares the Lord of them to the greatest," declares the Lord.

* 24 hours earlier

Nineteen-year-old Rita is on the dinner table with her seventeen-year-old sister Tina with their parents

Tina: "Mike is picking me up tomorrow evening to go see a movie and because it will be Friday night and no school the following day; I'll spend the night at his house.

Mom: "It's ok dear, your dad and I are going to a party, and we might not even come back home.

What about you Rita?

Sarcastic tone, Mom continues

Mom: "Do you have bible studies?"

Rita: "As a matter of fact, A sister from church, her name is Brunise! She will pick me up tomorrow so we can go on a Bible study with one of her co-workers.

Tina and mom laugh

Tina: "Why aren't we surprised?"

Dad: "You are laughing because she wants to do good, this is how crazy this world is"

Mom: "I was just laughing because we guessed in advance what she was going to do"

Dad: "I said Exactly what I meant to say"

Dad turns to Rita

Dad: "I am proud of what you do, dear! I envy you because I wish I could also do that"

Rita: "You can daddy, I asked you many times to study the Bible, but you refuse, there is no way you can do what I do if you are not in love with God."

Dad: "I have one daughter that is going to spend the night with her boyfriend and the other one is going to study the bible with others. That should not even be a choice."

Tina: "Are you ashamed of me, daddy?

Dad: "I am not ashamed of you honey and you know that. I love you and I just want you to be happy. That doesn't mean that I am going to like all your decisions."

Mom: "This conversation already took place and we all agreed it is better to be open about things Instead of having secrets."

Rita: "Dad, there is a scripture in the Bible that says * How then can you call on the one that you have not believed in?"

Mom: "Enough Rita, both you and your sister. Do what you want if you are happy"

Meanwhile a few miles away

28 years old Brunise is having dinner with her husband

Brunise: "I want to remind you that tomorrow afternoon, I will pick up my friend Rita and we are going to do a Bible study with one of my co-workers"

Glenn: "You already told me, and I remember, that's the reason after work some of us going to the bar and watch the basketball game"

Brunise: "You didn't say anything about you going to the bar"

Glenn: "2 years ago, you found God, I am not stopping you, but I don't like it because it's taking time away from us. We can watch church services on TV, and I will support you. We can do it together, but you go to church, Bible study, Bible talk and more. That is too much"

Brunise: "Everything you just said that I do. I pray that we do them together. The life of a Christian is not only Sunday but every day. Watching Church service on TV is entertainment and only that. Disciples of Jesus Christ don't only listen, we also get involved but you don't even want to study the Bible because if you do it and put your heart in it, you will also be in love with God."

Glenn: "I love you, that's the reason I stay, otherwise I would not be here"

Brunise: "I hope your love for me is strong enough one day for you to say I want to know God the way you know him"

Glenn: "Don't push it! Do what you want as long as you are happy"

Matthew 10:34-36 NIV

Do not suppose that I have come to bring peace to the earth. I did not come to bring peace, but a sword. For I have come to turn "'a man against his father, a daughter against her mother, a daughter-in-law against her mother-in-law— a man's enemies will be the members of his own household.

Disciples of Jesus Christ take captive every thought and make it obedient to God. We stand on faith, and it is a muscle, so we use it every day. Sin is a big dog and the way we control it is to make it weak by living in the Spirit. Our brother Paul said in

Romans 8: 6 NIV

The mind governed by the flesh is death, but the mind governed by the Spirit is life and peace.

As a Disciple of Christ, Evangelism and sharing our faith is not an optional accessory to our lives. It is our heartbeat. We are justified by the love of God, sanctified by the Holy Spirit, and saved by the blood of Jesus Christ. When we look at a Disciple of Christ, we are looking at the Holy Spirit because they are the temple and the physical body of the Spirit of Christ.

Every single day and all day long we have the fear of God which is: hope, loyalty, compassion, care, poise in chaos, wisdom, love and so much more. Every Disciple has an instructor to walk with. It is to help get Christ's disciples to look, talk and be like Jesus with the Holy Spirit as our guide.

What will the excuses be before the Lord: We didn't know? If only we knew?

Well, the time is now when we must decide. Discrimination, division is not a good action and cannot be part of the Church. We must do whatever it takes to be part of God's kingdom, we do not have time to waste because very soon the Lord will gather his people.

The ark of Noah is done, the Shepherd is gathering his Sheep. This is our time now, so this message is for the scattered Sheep that belong to the Sheep Pen, come home, and find a disciple of Christ to show you the way home. The Lord has reserved a remnant for himself and if you are part of it no matter where you are, He will find you.

The devil will not stop coming after us. That's what he does, and we do not expect anything less from him. We must always be on our guard because so many of us were fired up for the Lord and now they are no longer because they chose things from this world instead of God.

The decision is like day or night, God of this world, your sinful desire for flesh or the Spirit of God.

The Word of God is very dangerous if we don't apply it in our life. The same Word that can save our lives will condemn and destroy them. We need to be patient, stay faithful, be strong and take heart to the end and wait for the Lord, otherwise when the storm comes, we will be destroyed.

Apostle Paul in his letters, always wanted us to understand the urgency and the conviction that we must have because serving God cannot be second in our lives but must always be first. From our everyday life we should understand a little bit of the great gift that God has given us. We are justified by God after baptizing, sanctified by the Holy Spirit and Saved by the blood of Jesus Christ

Because of our faith, we are saved through his grace, but we need to keep moving in steps with the Spirit he gave us otherwise we will stay behind. There are no such things: "Once saved always saved"

That is something the devil wants you to believe. Did you pray and read the Bible today and every day? How could you have a relationship with the Lord if you don't get on your knees and humble yourself every morning when you wake up?

You need to be Holy (separate yourself from this world), be like Jesus and live your life like he did. The world will soon be destroyed but if you don't choose God, you will be destroyed with it.

The Spirit that you have will guide you and help you so you can be transformed in his likeness.

Does God have a claim on you or do you belong to the devil?

Do not seek money but seek God, do not seek happiness but seek God instead, do not seek good health but seek God instead.... By reading this book, God is already calling on you to seek him with all your heart to find him and when you do! You will find out what true love is. Yes, I am calling on you to love God before yourself, your spouse, and your children.

Do you or don't you? Only you know that answer! So if not... Do you want to?

God wants to confirm you to the image of his Son Jesus Christ.

My wife

It is extremely important for a Christian to marry someone with the same beliefs otherwise most likely the marriage will not last. I love my wife so every single day, I must remember the Scriptures say that we must love our wives as Christ loves the Church.

Self-control, humility, and forgiveness are what I keep praying for everyday in order for God to make our marriage perfect in his sight.

I learned self-discipline, something that I could not ever achieve if I were still a part of the world. I value what she values and choose humility instead of pride. The solution is to start wanting what God wants. As a godly man that wants to please God, it makes it easy to do even though Satan is trying to confuse us with pride and defensiveness. Anger is a reaction then our sinful nature takes over. As a husband and a leader of my household, I am an example for my spouse and with the love that I have for Christ and my wife, I know that we are walking in steps with the Spirit.

Difficulties and bad things will continue to happen not only in our marriage but to everybody because there is so much evil in the world. We know that we must never respond in a sinful way no matter how bad things are. It is sin that enslaves our heart and destroys our character.

Always seeking God every day in order not to let deceit or bad attitudes overtake our hearts.

Our marriage is not a string of 2 but of 3 because God is always there so therefore, we do not let our past, our hardships, difficulties and surroundings control us. We trust God above our experiences.

I am a disciple of Jesus Christ, I am a husband, I am a man of my word, I am a man of noble character, I have self-control, self-discipline. I set my mind on things above, I work on my marriage with scriptures and love our differences. I know that I am blessed because many are called but few are chosen. My wife is a princess, she is God's child so therefore not only that the Lord is my father he is also my father-in-law. My mission is also to encourage my wife and make her radiant.

My Son

The saying is true. Children follow their parents' example so when I became a Christian, my seventeen years old son also studied the Bible with other Christians and fell in love with God just like I did and became a disciple of Jesus Christ.

Weeks earlier, I received a call from his school because he was fighting with another kid for marijuana. Once he became a disciple, he took his Bible at school to help others understand the plan that God has for all of us.

Unfortunately, after graduation he went out of state and could not stay in step with the Spirit.

I pray for him every day that one day he will have the opportunity to come back to the wonderful kingdom of God.

The most radical thing a person can do is to stay consistent.

Our friend at the time witnessed the changes in both my son and me so when I asked him to have a Bible study; he said no way because he didn't want to change like we did.

Most people will say "no" when a Christian asks them to study the Bible because once they realize the truth, the choice will be clear to either keep living as they are or make a drastic change. We cannot become Christian and still live like a non Christian because that is impossible.

Can someone serve God 99 percent? No, impossible! The kingdom Jesus came to establish, and its message is the only way for salvation. The devil is confusing people by letting them know that they are already saved when they are not. I encourage you to work hard and always give the best of yourself and learn from the mistakes you will make. Remember my son and always remember, please! We are like grass in this world and soon we will be no more but if you have the fear of God, you will obey him and follow his commands therefore your rewards are for you to live forever in his presence; You were once my spiritual brother, so you know how it is to love and have the fear of God. It is something that we cannot just tell people, they must open the Bible and walk on that beautiful narrow path. I hope that by my example and with the Lord's blessings, soon you will be back fishing as a fisher of men. I reminisce when we were out sharing our faith with people and asked them if they wanted to study the Bible.

The road to God is narrow but the other one is wide open. Don't ignore this warning by keeping living your life without the fear of God so do not give away your authority that Jesus gives to anyone that does his Heavenly father's will. The scripture says that Lord our God, the Lord is one.

MY DAUGHTER

My 15 years old daughter! What can a father who is a servant of the living God pray for everyday? For his daughter to have the fear of God and love him with all her heart and nothing else.

I can write thousands of pages just on what is the fear of God that I am seeking for you, my daughter.

You are at an intersection called life right now and soon you will have to turn right or left. I can no longer carry you on my shoulders, I must put you down so you can choose this world or the word of God.

Flesh or Spirit, life or death! That's all.

To fear God, you must love him and to love him you must know him.

The heart is where it must start because to do that it must be humble, obedient, loving and seeking God.

You have all these qualities, but the deceiver is stronger than you, but God is above all so whoever is seeking God will find him.

Just like my life is an example of what God's glory can do; I want the same for you. Always work hard on your relationship with God because that's what he desires from you. The greatest gift in the world is to know and have a relationship with God. Please not like the way the world worshipped God but the way the disciples from the first century church worshipped him and that is the greatest gift that I can show you and it is yours if you want it.

I want you to imagine my beautiful daughter as a princess being born with everything that is from this world already being handed to her. At the same time a poor girl from the poorest country in the world is also being born but God rejoices for the poor baby girl because he knows the latter has her name written in the book of life. Be smart in this world, we are going through labor so your satisfaction should only be when you help others to escape the grip of the ruler of this world, who is the devil. Very soon the children of God will be revealed and creation itself waits in eager expectation for this to happen.

Do not follow people but follow the word of God instead. His expectation is for us to bear fruit so you must set yourself apart to do what others don't or won't do.

Know God, love God and let the Holy Spirit guide you. I told you and I am warning you again, this world does not belong to God, it has a king, and it is satan. Escape for the Lord to set you apart and there is no other way. Can someone get hit by a train and still look the same?

The People that call themselves Christians these days look the same as the people that call themselves atheists. At your young age, you already know the difference and I don't need to say anymore except that I love you and pray that soon I can call you my spiritual sister. I hope that you follow your heart and always do what you believe is right by including God in all your decisions. I am so blessed to be your father and thank God for you. No matter how hard or unpredictable life is if you stay faithful to God, I know you will be okay because in all things God works for the good of the people that love him.

Andree

What do you expect a twenty-year-old college man to do? Act like a twenty-year-old college man of course so anything different is odd and unusual.

When one day he was met with a Christ disciple; He believed, repented and got baptized. He went home and his parents saw that drastic change because he was praying and reading the bible; that's what we do when we are in love with God.

We want to please him by doing his will, which is making more disciples so they can also be a part of the kingdom of God for them to do the same.

His parents thought that he was in a cult of course, which was their first thought, so they went to find out what's going on with that organization.

Months later the whole family got baptized and became disciples of Jesus Christ.

Hassiem

My name is Hassiem and I've been a Christian for almost five years. It's been a complicated, challenging yet powerful walk with God and I've not been bored at any moment at all. The story of me becoming a Christian is unique. I had the honor of getting baptized and forgiven by the Lord on November 20th, 2016. I became a Christian by accident. In college I studied dramatic arts and my dream growing up was to become an actor. Since I was twelve years old, I have had the gift of connecting with audiences through plays and various mediums. In fact, I've also done stand-up comedy and in Junior college in 2014 I won the audience choice award.

When I entered college in University of California Irvine, I had my entertainment career all set up and ready to go. I began to worry about my future graduating after college because I realized that many people were graduating and having trouble finding jobs or they were in fields that they didn't even enjoy. I was cold marketing trying to make rent then I met a Christian. I asked her, "Would you be interested in making extra money?" She said, "No but would you like to come to church?" I replied "Yes I need church because my life is not going well, and I need some serious help. At this point I met real loving Christians who showed serious concern about my life, I was not used to that.

I was introduced to the first principles studies, and I realized very quickly that I was not a disciple of Jesus Christ therefore, not a Christian and not Saved. I learned how to apply the bible in life, and I was cut to heart by the scriptures. Then I got baptized and was forgiven by the Lord for my sins. Making disciples while sharing God-given creativity is now my new purpose in life.

We must have faith, repent, be baptized and do the same to others. We must rely on God's love for us because God is love! We live in love! Love for the lost and love for one another, otherwise God is not in us. When we are not living in love for one another and the lost. God doesn't connect or relate to us. God's love is seen through our living in the Spirit!

BRENDON

A Tale of Three Kings Reflection

There was once a man who led his people and sought to do what was right, even when it hurt him. He did not seek praise from man, but later received from God what was promised. This man had every opportunity to retaliate against his persecutors. This man was King David; a man whom I wish to imitate as he foreshadowed the coming of the perfect King, Jesus. After reading the Tale of Three Kings, by Gene Edwards, I learned of the types of leadership that help me be a better leader in God's kingdom. I am inspired that I could lead my Bible talk in a way that imitates David's humility and wins people from all walks of life.

Leadership is a huge topic that I have always internally wanted, yet never believed that I would obtain, until I entered the kingdom. I believed that I would live a standard "good" life and was anything but humble, believing that I could not do wrong and could get away with anything. I could attribute this attitude to my childhood, as I did not have many people who believed in me. Unlike David, I grew up as an only child, and was spoiled in many ways:

My family always sheltered me and gave me almost anything I wanted, and I was rarely left to think about how to solve anything. When I was finally reached out to, my attitude and pride were brought down to the ground as I went through the studies. I saw how I lived a self-centered life and how I was in fact imitating Saul as opposed to David. I was easily irritable, envious, and unloving in both my words, lack of words, and deeds, much like 2 Timothy 3:1-5 describes. Now living as a disciple of Jesus, I am moved to live a David-like life that honors Christ and His people. I found a family that believed in me and was with me through thick and thin and was entrusted with a small team of my own to cultivate and cherish: the HD campus Bible talk.

Leadership of a small, diverse group is the exact way that Jesus changed the world! By focusing on these few, time and effort can be directed into them to raise them up and teach them to obey. It was not until my second year as a Christian that I started to understand the impact of this teaching, it is through these small groups that disciples can multiply and win people from all nations. Upon reading a Tale of Three Kings, I realized that this was the type of group that followed king David, a ragtag band of outcasts and those looking for change. This describes us as disciples and how God can use common people like me to painfully advance the kingdom! One recent instance that struck a chord of the toil it is to add to a Bible talk would be studying with other people:

We are studying with a young man who has several health challenges that affect his character, though he has a heart to seek after God. We recently did all the studies with him, but it was revealed that he had some things he was holding back, which hurt us. After much prayer and advice, we are resolved to continue to help him according to his needs, knowing that the Word will not return empty. It is only thanks to a David-like imitation rooted in the Word that has helped me to endure hardships like this!

How inspiring it is that I could lead my Bible talk in a way that imitates David's humility and changes people from all nations! Despite my past, God has given me the humility to seek Him and lead His people in a way that glorifies Him. This leadership can then be instilled within our Bible talks and then into the people around us, thus adding to God's kingdom. I cannot wait to see how God will add to every aspect of our Bible talk we **choose** to imitate.

WHO AM I?

I am grateful. I AM a child of God. I AM redeemed from the hand of the enemy. I AM forgiven. I AM saved by grace through faith. I AM justified. I AM a new creature in Christ. I AM a partaker of divine nature. I AM redeemed from the curse of the law. I am grateful. I AM delivered from the powers of darkness. I AM led by the spirit of God. I AM a son of God. I AM kept in safety wherever I go. I AM getting all my needs met by Jesus. I AM casting all my cares on Jesus. I AM strong in the Lord and in the power of His might. I AM doing all things through Christ who strengthens me. I AM heir of God and a joint heir with Jesus. I AM heir to the blessing of Abraham. I AM observing and doing the Lord's commandments. I AM blessed coming in and going out. I am grateful. I AM an inheritor of eternal life. I AM blessed with all spiritual blessings. I AM healed by His stripes. I AM exercising my authority over the enemy. I AM above and not beneath. I AM more than a conqueror. I AM establishing God's Word here on earth. I AM an overcomer by the blood of the lamb and my testimony. I AM overcoming the devil. I AM not moved by what I see. I AM walking by faith and not by sight. I AM casting down vain imaginations. I AM bringing every thought into captivity. I AM being transformed by a renewed mind. I AM a laborer together with God. I AM the righteousness of God in Christ Jesus. I AM an imitator of Jesus. I AM a light to the world, and I AM complete with Christ. I AM God's workmanship, created in Christ Jesus for good works that God prepared for me to walk in. I AM blessed. I AM seated in heavenly places with Christ. I AM a saint, and I AM a disciple of Christ because I love others. I AM victorious and I AM alive with Christ. I AM loved with an everlasting love. I AM set free, and I always triumph in Christ. I AM crucified with Christ. I AM His faithful follower. I AM being changed into His image. I AM one in Christ. I have an abundant life and I press toward the goal. I live by the law of the Holy Spirit. I AM born of God and the evil one does not touch me. I AM the apple of my Father's eye. My God is faithful, and I am reaping the harvest of all God's promises. I AM pleasing God and doing His will. I AM grateful.

I am a disciple of Jesus Christ; I am an ambassador from the Kingdom of God.

Yes, I am only here for a little while because soon people will not see me any longer unless they become my spiritual brothers and sisters. The time is coming when if I needed some water to drink, the homes of my daughter or my son will not even be safe for me if they are not my sister and brother in Christ (Believe, Repent and Be Baptized)

How could that be? I see past difficulties for what they are and see God's blessings instead.

I always depend on God even if my Soul is full of trouble. Lately I have been praying more deeply than ever before because prayer is the key to overcome feelings that may seem overpowering. Not growing on our faith? The answer is because you are not praying the way you should, which is to give glory to God, confess your sins, give thanks to God and a humble request because we are not worthy of his love for us.

The glory days are now! Our willingness will sustain us through prayers.

As a Christ disciple, there is no excuse for me to sin against God no matter what evil or trouble comes upon me. I know who the enemy is and keep my heart soft through God's love therefore the deceiver cannot harm me because God is with me.

Knowing that God wants everything in our hearts to be revealed for him to make the changes including our feelings and memories about the past.

The peace that I have in God is greater than my feelings. Satan's scheme is to keep us trapped in unhappiness, but God has a different plan for us if we only let him in.

Can you imagine living every day the way God had planned it? God detailed the plan; we must execute it by being in step with God.

The way of Christianity is Jesus, as his Disciples we get to prepare the way for him.

We are part of his kingdom and with Jesus as our King and reigning in Heaven, we know that the king of this world will never prevail over us if we stay true to God and stay under his rulership. We are a citizen in Heaven functioning on earth as an ambassador of Jesus with one mission of bringing lost souls to him.

We are blessed and we want you to see what to see and to know what we know.

Religion and Kingdom are two different things. The first one is a particular system of beliefs and the other one is a territory or government ruled by a king. The focus of Jesus' teaching is his Kingdom. Disciples do not have a religion or denomination but have citizenship in the Kingdom of God.

When we bow down to pray, we are talking to our King because in a kingdom the subjects are supposed to do that before their kings and we read the Bible, our King is talking to us and these are acts that we must do every day in order to stay under his grace because the ruler of this world is looking for every opportunity to take us back when we already been bought with the blood our Lord Jesus Christ. The weapons we fight with are not from this world.

LORD Jesus, people think of "Lord" in a religious way but in a kingdom the king is also the Lord because he owns everything inside his kingdom and our LORD Jesus owns us because we belong to him. The Royal's law of our King is to love our God with all our hearts and our neighbors as ourselves.

I chose to stop being manipulated by the deceiver. The great power that God has given me is more powerful than what the king of this world has. The decision is to let God's word comfort me. My sins, attitudes and feelings that plagued me can be destroyed through God's word.

The difference is obvious for the people that lived godly or ungodly lives.

Ephesians 6:12-13 NIV

For our struggle is not against flesh and blood, but against the rulers, against the authorities, against the powers of this dark world and against the spiritual forces of evil in the heavenly realms. Therefore, put on the full armor of God, so that when the day of evil comes, you may be able to stand your ground, and after you have done everything, to stand.

We are resurrected to a new life therefore we are no longer citizens of this world but Ambassadors. Our King expects Devotion.

People are looking or searching for happiness but only in God will they be able to find it but unfortunately most of them don't believe that.

Darkness is the absence of light; people hate the light so we must show them (the one that is willing to listen) the only way people can understand the light is because of God's guidance.

We know that our Lord is also our Shepherd, our light, our Savior and our Peace. Our Job is to bring Scattered Sheep to him just as he commanded us to do on the Great Commission.

Revelation 3:17 NIV

You say, 'I am rich; I have acquired wealth and do not need a thing.' But you do not realize that you are wretched, pitiful, poor, blind and naked.

Disciples of Christ approach God with confidence because we know in Christ nothing holds us back and are fully assured in faith. We pray and read the Bible every day as a result God shines in our heart. What we don't have is hatred because we know that is an enslaving sin.

Love God is to obey His commands. Discipling helps our hearts to want to obey His commands

Jesus's command is to teach them to obey everything and surely, he is with us to the very end of the age.

Therefore, we must love one another by lying down our lives for each other if needs be just like our Lord did for us.

We know who we are, but we also know where we are. Therefore, we are very grateful and humble servants of our Lord that blessed us, forgave our transgressions and covered our sins forever if we stayed loyal servants.

We don't hold sins inside. We confess to one another and to God and as a result Satan does not have a piece of us. Evil thoughts, hatred, malice, envy, lust and all types of evil, we don't hide from them, we confront them because only God is the answer.

True joy comes from God even in affliction, troubles or death. We rejoice every day because we decide to be righteous and live a righteous life.

Comfort comes from Christ so we can help others. Disciples make themselves, their bodies a living sacrifice before God as a result He uses one another to help each other.

As Christians, hating, lack of forgiveness or any sin is no longer an option because we know those things will destroy our ability to have faith and stay faithful to God. When one person decides to live for God that means that person chooses life.

Satan's scheme to keep us trapped in unhappiness or give us the illusion of happiness.

Hurt and bitterness bring out unnecessary pride that blocks God and enables Satan to reign in our lives.

God wants everything in our hearts to be revealed. Confess our sins to God and to each other, be blameless and transparent just like our Lord Jesus was on this earth.

When deep resentment and bitterness are exposed, we are often tempted to hide them out of shame and pride but focusing on God pulls us through and helps us to be righteous.

Everything in life is a decision so let God's word guide and comfort us so we can get the power to overcome the enemy-satan.

Our sins, our attitudes and our feelings that plague us can be destroyed through God's word.

We choose the Bible as our ultimate guide even when it hurts. In doing that we can say "Yes" with confidence to the question below.

Who may ascend the mountain of the Lord?

Who may stand in his holy place?

Christ made us worthy.

Election night:

Such a delicate matter that we don't talk much about; No matter who got your vote or didn't; Does not really matter because God is searching for our hearts.

There cannot be no division so we must start there. I have people that I love from the church that will never vote for a particular party and another group of people feel the same way about the other party. Are you willing to judge? Please step forward so the whole assembly can look at you.

The church is a hospital for sinners because it is the sick who need a doctor. The Holy Spirit helps us understand the love of God and of his Son Jesus Christ. But this type of division is beyond my understanding, I needed more wisdom, and the answer must be in the Bible.

The first to speak in a lawsuit is always right until someone else comes and cross-examines.

I voted and I went to a spiritual brother's house so we can pray and share our love for God on election night, but no one asked, "Who did you vote for?" We are a conservative church so of course automatically we are on the same page. Aren't we? I realize now! Will apostle Paul be a part of separation?

We assume to know the party that our Lord wants to win. I voted so why do I feel guilty? There is something in my heart that is not right so for me to have clean hands and a pure heart, I know now what I must do.

2 Timothy 2:4 NIV

No one serving as a soldier gets entangled in civilian affairs, but rather tries to please his commanding officer.

I will make mistakes, but I will learn from my mistakes. From now on I will let the Spirit of Jesus guide me in every aspect of my life, it is clear like pure water. Here am I. Send me my Lord! When I am with my brothers and sisters, I will not feel guilty but have clean hands and a pure heart no matter who they voted for because I am not a civilian.

A day in the life of a Christ's Disciple

I woke up this morning, but I did not feel alone. I got on my knees, prayed to the Lord and read the Bible. I got up to brush my teeth and right there in the mirror, I was staring at myself, someone that I am very familiar with. I was thinking about my children, my wife, siblings, all the people that love me and that I also love. I would give my life here for them but the Spirit that is inside me is there to separate me from most of them.

I asked most of them many times to study the Bible with me, but they think that I am strange, and they are fine just the way they are. I have hope that one day they will catch up and see what I see, feel what I feel and love God the way I love God. I must keep moving forward with the Spirit that is inside me. What is inside me? I am covered with the fear of the Lord and Love resides inside me.

I know that I am blessed because my transgressions are forgiven, and God has covered my sins. He wants me to be an example of what his glory can do because before he found me, I was a street dog without a purpose. Now I am God's ambassador in this world.

I am aware every day about how far I've come from those terrible days of the past. I will continue to trust in God and rejoice in my salvation. Every single day is a new battle so I will keep fighting with God by my side so I can get rid of any deceit that is left in my heart for God to completely heal me.

My Lord Jesus was tempted to be resentful and bitter, but he stayed faithful to the end. God helped him to overcome it.

Jesus is the perfect disciple of God that we are imitating.

John 15:9-10 NIV

As the father has loved me, so have I loved you. Now remain in my love. If you keep my commands, you will remain in my love, just as I have kept my father's commands and remain in his love.

No matter what, I must always put my trust in God because I know that I am already passing from darkness to light in my life through love.

I think about the people in my life that I love but are unable to completely love or give their hearts to because they are not really convinced of God's love for them.

Bad events or hardships somehow convinced them that God does not care. They fail to understand the need to put their trust completely in God despite their hopes not coming to fruition.

My family doesn't know how lucky I am, in fact they think that I am part of a cult. Jesus's human family thought he was out of his mind and that is the way this world sees the children of God. In the church, we are surrounded by the people who love and respect us no matter what.

Because of my past hurts, many things have attacked my body, my mind and my self-esteem. But God has given us his Son whose blood has washed away all the past and in time will even wash away my bad memory. Life's challenges are not necessarily a curse from God therefore I must keep my faith in God through the good and bad.

One Saturday afternoon, about 2 dozen disciples gathered at the airport to welcome one of our disciple brothers coming back from a very fruitful mission trip. While moving down the escalator, we started singing!

What a beautiful sight to be a part of God's church and be one of his children! Everyone is looking, smiling and envious a little bit.

They don't understand, we want them so much to be a part of the family so they can be our brothers and sisters but there is only one way: "Lets pray then open the Bible on Psalms 119: 1-2"

Escape & Welcome to the Kingdom of God!

MY CHILDREN IN THE FAITH

I believe children pay attention to their parents' advice better when they are dead instead of alive, so I wanted to write a warning letter for you to read after I am gone, rejoice I am still with you but pay attention. Most everyone you know is the same, there is no difference. The people that go to church and the people that don't. I am warning you right now my children; they are all the same! God will judge our hearts and our actions so we must escape Satan's scheme against us. I am going to call on you to be holy and do not settle for anything else.

Revelation 22:11 NIV

Let the one who does wrong continue to do wrong; let the vile person continue to be vile; let the one who does right continue to do right; and let the holy person continue to be holy.

Jesus really came to this world, died for our sins, resurrected and he is coming back soon.

The whole world is under Satan's control, but God always sets a few people apart for himself and before Christ came to this world, it was the Jewish people. Imagine all nations in the world, he picked only one nation and called them his people, but they rejected him so God's people are no longer a physical nation but a spiritual nation that whoever wants to follow the teaching of Jesus Christ can be part of that kingdom. A Christian life is a life of training that must live within healthy emotional boundaries and that is the essence of the disciplined Christian life. Overcoming evil with good and being successful at battling self-pity. Believe only what is written in the Bible. There are many false doctrines that are being preached and these people are not doing the will of God, they are not making disciples, they are not teaching people how to be disciples of Jesus Christ and be saved. They are entertainers, that's all. They are like Balaam (Refuted by a Donkey) they think they have a relationship with God but not living according to God's will. Ask any Christians if they are Disciples of Christ and they will say 'yes' but they don't realize a disciple is a student so therefore they must do the will of the teacher which is our king Jesus. The world is corrupt. Do not trust any preachers or anyone that comes to you if they are not disciples of Jesus Christ. You will know who they are by their actions because Christ's Disciples are humble, loving, gentle and want to please God. They will instruct you in the word of God, baptize you in the name of the Father, Son and Holy Spirit so you can become one of them for you to go and do the same. Disciples are called "chosen people, a royal priesthood, a holy nation and God's special possession" Do not follow false doctrines but rejoice always in the Lord. Every single answer should be in the bible so do not let people interpret scriptures. Do not believe in the writings of the false prophets because they all teach the same lie which is "I received a message from God". Can you add anything to perfection? The Lord has made his message plain for everybody to understand but people want to justify their evil behavior by interpreting scriptures when it's elementary for anyone who wants to move out of the darkness and walk to the light in order to have a relationship with God. These people still crawl on the floor, they are only drinking milk.

The scriptures say if you live on milk, you are an infant and not acquainted with righteousness, but solid food is for the people that are constantly training themselves about the word of God.

Return good for evil; I know it's easier said than done but the Lord knows that it's not easy. That is the reason once you accept him as your savior then after being baptized, our Lord will give you the gift of the Holy Spirit to guide you all the days of your life here. We are restoring the first century church so any preaching after the book of revelation in the bible is false teaching so do not entertain those people. Just like the disciples in the first century were persecuted, killed for their faith so you must be on your guard and stay alert because the time is coming when you might have to choose between this world or Jesus, I am not writing figuratively. The message Disciples preach turns people's lives upside down because they realize to serve God they have to work and it's not possible to go to church only on Sunday, even if they pray every day and think that they have a relationship with God; it takes much more than that.

A disciple is a worker, always wanting to please his master by praying and reading the bible every day, studying with people, teaching them, baptizing them. Bible talk, midweek service, activities, have fun together and give glory to God always. One Church, One King, One God and One family.

Satan and his children will make us think otherwise but Disciples of Christ follow the king and live for him and when we sin, we can always go before him and ask for forgiveness.

1 John 3:1 NIV

See what great love the Father has lavished on us, that we should be called children of God! And that is what we are! The reason the world does not know us is that it did not know him.

From beginning to the end there is no greater title than to be a "Servant of the living God"

The world calls us strange and different and yes, we are because we are not one of them.

They did not recognize our Lord in fact, they killed him! Be ready to die for him if need be and always remember our body is a living sacrifice to God and we are the temple of the Holy Spirit.

To love God is to obey His commands. Discipling helps our hearts to want to obey His commands

Ask the so-called Christians they don't even know what discipling is and they say that they are followers of Jesus, so I am begging you to escape.

John 15:18-19 NIV

If the world hates you, keep in mind that it hated me first. If you belonged to the world, it would love you as its own. As it is, you do not belong to the world, but I have chosen you out of the world. That is why the world hates you.

Escape my children!!!

With Love,

Your dad in the faith

To:

The scattered Sheep,

I was one of you until God put his servant on my path to find my way home. Listen to the message from the good Shepherd so you too can find your way home.

There are two types of people so which one are you?

John 10:26-27 NIV

. . . but you do not believe it because you are not my sheep. My sheep listen to my voice; I know them, and they follow me.

Jeremiah 7:27 NIV

When you tell them all this, they will not listen to you; when you call them, they will not answer.

Therefore, without a doubt you know who you are

Proverbs 9:7-8 NIV

Whoever corrects a mocker invites insults; whoever rebukes the wicked incurs abuse. Do not rebuke mockers or they will hate you; rebuke the wise and they will love you.

P.S. The movement is moving with or without you, but one thing is for sure you won't have any excuses. The Great Escape is a reference book backed up by scriptures. Restoring the first century Church, the Shepherd is calling his Sheep so just like it was on the day of Noah; the animals are being assembled to go inside the Arc.

ABOUT THE AUTHOR

The Great Escape, by Daniel Jean-Louis, an author that nobody knows has the potential to change the Christianity religions for generations. It is indeed a testimony to God on how he uses the dimmest to shine on and make them the brightest for his glory.

Mr. Jean-Louis, Haitian born and immigrated to the United States in 1984, did not do anything extraordinary in his writings. He simply let the scriptures speak for themselves.

Romans 1: 19 NIV "Since what may be known about God is plain to them, because God has made it plain to them"

The Great Escape is a reference book backed by scriptures for Christianity religions.

Understanding repentance and what it means to live a lifestyle of it. Repentance is a grace of God's Spirit whereby a sinner is inwardly humbled and visibly changed.

Thousands of churches but there can only be one. The Great Escape wants us to go to the teachings of the original Church that started at Pentecost.

Recognize our sin, be sorrowful, confess it, be ashamed of it, hatred of sin and turn from sin. In doing so the blood of Jesus will set us free in order to live our lives as Jesus did. We will be part of the Kingdom of God and will be called "Children of God

ESCAPE

I am a Disciple of Christ; you can find us if you are seeking God with all your heart. Our Lord Jesus said that his gospel will be preached all over the world before he comes back. It is happening now! We are asking you to study the bible, we are knocking at your door and you can even go on our website. No matter where you are in the world God can put his servant on your path. Do you really want to escape?

www.cityofangelsicc.org

Printed in the United States
by Baker & Taylor Publisher Services